To Calvin

THE TWO-DOLLAR BOAT

The Two-Dollar Boat

Boat Stories and

Other Lies

by Dudley B. Magruder, Jr.

Illustrated by
Stacy Cates,
Rebecca Magruder,
and Robbie Lockridge

FITHIAN PRESS · SANTA BARBARA · 1992

To Gail Madden
Writing a book is hard work. For me it would be impossible without the help of a patient, competent, and supportive assistant. I couldn't do without Gail.

Book design and typography by Jim Cook

LIBRARY OF CONGRESS CATALOGING-IN-PUBLICATION DATA
Magruder, Dudley B. (Dudley Boston), 1914–
    The two-dollar boat and other adventures / Dudley B.
Magruder.
        p. cm.
    ISBN 156474-000-5
    1. Boats and boating—Anecdotes. I. Title.
GV777.3.M34   1992   91-24247
797.1—dc 20   CIP

Contents

Introduction 7

The Two-Dollar Boat 9

Steamboating on the Coosa 18

Queen of the Ferry 31

Sailing with Ernie 40

Airborne 45

The P-G Special 54

The *Good Omen* 60

Voyage of the *Fat Girl* 68

Get the Anchor Down 79

Escape from Soddy Daisy 93

Starboard, Dammit! 100

Off the Coast of Maine 106

"I Was in the Channel" 120

All Girl Crew 131

The Rope Ladder 141

Dinner at Plato's 149

Introduction

I'M SORRY THE BOOK IS FINISHED—writing it has been a lot of fun. The lady who did the editing asked me if the stories were true. Well, now, some of them are mostly true and some are partly true and some are only a little bit true and on some, I dunno. The people were fun to do. Like the stories, some of them are mostly true and all of them ought to be true whether I knew them personally or not. I liked them all, from Billy Bob, who drifted over the dam, to Linda, the waitress whose name wasn't really Linda, to Dr. Poovey, who still made house calls. I hope you will like them, too.

I wish to acknowledge that I am indebted to a number of sources and a number of people, including *A History of Rome and Floyd County* by George Magruder Battey; *All Roads to Rome* by Roge Aycock; Sandra Sentell, Paul Shiflett, and Dianne Cumming, who provided useful information; and Suzanne Shiflett Jones, who edited the whole manuscript for me.

I'm thinking about some stories about old lawyers, but I dunno.

DUDLEY B. MAGRUDER, JR.

Rome, Georgia
May 1991

The Two-Dollar Boat

THE MUDDY OLD BATEAU was tied to an overhanging limb. There was a man sitting on one of the seats. I didn't see any fishing canes or anything in the boat except an old homemade paddle and a Maxwell House coffee can. He must have heard me come up because he looked up and smiled. It was a nice smile. He said, "Hello, sonny. Does your mother know you're down here on the riverbank?"

"No, sir. I doubt if she does. I'm a good swimmer though. I can swim across the country club pool at least twice without stopping."

He sort of snorted. "Country club, huh? Rich folks."

"No, sir. We're not rich. My father works for an insurance company, and we live right over the hill from here—and I come down on the riverbank a lot."

"Sonny, you look like a nice boy and you need to be mighty careful. This ain't no country club pool. This is the old Etowah River; she's crooked, muddy, and full of snags. Sometimes the water gets up and the current gets real fast; you could get drowned in here mighty easy—you need to be real careful."

I was a polite young boy. I said, "Yes, sir. I'll be real careful. Is the water cold?"

"I don't know," he said. "I doubt if it's too cold yet. You're not planning on going swimming in here are you?"

"No, sir. I just wondered in case I were to fall in. You doing any fishing, sir?" I ventured.

"Why, no. I don't fish much anymore. Nothing in the river anyway except catfish and a few carp. I don't mind eatin' catfish, but carp's got too many bones. They just too much trouble to eat. I just come down here to get away and think about things. It's nice and peaceful, and you don't see many people."

We both thought about things for a while. He blew a smoke ring and then blew a little smoke ring right through the big one.

"Ever see anybody do that?" he said.

"Why, no. No, I haven't. My father smokes, but I don't think he can blow smoke rings."

"Sometime I can blow a smoke ring and blow two little smoke rings through it, but it's hard to do. You have to practice a lot, and there can't be any wind."

He kept smoking and blowing rings, and I thought he might have forgotten I was there. Finally he said, "Folks call me Billy Bob. Never really liked it, but it seemed to sort of go with being a small man. Things don't always go too good when you're a

10

runt. My father owned a big farm in Vann's Valley, but my brother and sisters beat me out of my share. I was the youngest and the smallest, and they gave me a hard time. Now my old woman gives me a hard time—on my back all the time. I used to be a loom fixer at the cotton mill, but my health went bad, and I can't do nuthin' much anymore. The old woman thinks I'm puttin' on and that I'm just lazy. That ain't so. My back hurts nearly all the time. She was a good lookin' woman when I married her, but now she's fat and ugly. Works up there at the hosiery mill on 6th Avenue and complains all the time. Sheee! Mean, she's evermore mean. Sometime I think she may take it into her head to git rid of me. She's mainly the reason I come down here on the river—to get away from things. Sonny, folks tell me that this river runs all through Alabama and down to the ocean. Sometimes I think I'll just sit in this boat and drift all the way down to wherever it goes. I've really never been anywhere anyway. I guess the current would take me away from here."

"Mr. Billy Bob, I think this river does go down to the ocean, but I don't think you can get there that easy. I've heard there are dams and rocks and things, and anyway I think it's a long, long way."

I admired the old bateau. It was old and dirty, but it was a boat, and I wanted a boat really bad.

"Mr. Billy Bob, I know you love your boat, but I wonder if you would think about selling it."

"Who would I sell it to? You're too young to own a boat, and besides, I need to have some place to come."

He seemed to think for a while and made up a cigarette out of paper and tobacco he was carrying in a little sack in his shirt pocket.

My father smoked Chesterfields. They were nice smooth white cigarettes, not like the ones Billy Bob made. He rolled it and licked it, but it still didn't look like much. It did smoke, though, and he started blowing smoke rings again.

"This is a pretty good old boat. Been around a while and

leaks a little. Guess I'd have to have at least two dollars for it.''
I was excited now. "I've got two dollars in my drawer at home. I can run back over the hill and get it right now.''

"I don't know, sonny. I don't know whether I ought to sell you a boat. I know your mother wouldn't like it, and your daddy might give me a hard time if he finds out. It's worth two dollars, and I would throw in the paddle and the bailing can. You'd need to get you a padlock and some chain. Folks steal mighty bad on the river. You wouldn't have this boat long if you didn't take care of it.''

I was on my way. My mother was in the kitchen singing at the top of her voice. She didn't sing very well, but she seemed to enjoy it. She heard me come in and called out, ''Where you been?''

"Just been out playing. I'm going back out for a while. I'll be home in plenty of time for supper.''

"Well, be careful and don't stay out too long.''

I found my two dollars; most of it was in change, and I counted it again to make sure. When I got back to the river, Mr. Billy Bob was still there, and I counted the money out in his hand.

"I'm going to miss this old boat. I'll see how I do without it. Maybe I can do just as well coming down and sittin' on the riverbank. I know I can't stay home too much.'' He didn't offer to get out, but just kept sitting there.

"I've got to go home now,'' I said. "Please tie the boat up good, and I'll come down tomorrow and try it out.''

"You're going to have to have a better paddle than this one,'' he said. "This boat is terrible hard to paddle anyway, and this piece of board don't work too well.''

I had to go home before my mother started looking for me. I hated to leave and hoped that the boat would be all right. Mr. Billy Bob was still sitting in it when I left. He would have to find himself a place on the riverbank to sit because he'd sold me the boat. It was mine, and I intended to paddle it up and down the river.

ﻬ

There used to be an island near where Fifth Avenue ended at the Etowah River. It wasn't much of an island, but the river ran on both sides of it. That made it a genuine island like the ones I had read about. I thought maybe in a few days I would paddle over to the island and start making a hut. I couldn't camp out overnight because my mother would want to know where I was, but it would be nice to have a hut on an island and a boat so that I could get to it. I didn't think the island had a name so I would have to think up a name to call it.

The next day I got my friend Ernie to go with me. The boat was still where Billy Bob had left it, but it had a good bit of water in it. Ernie was a real neat boy, but he couldn't swim too well. "It's awful muddy," he said. "I don't think I'd better get in it. If I come home with a lot of mud, I will be in trouble. I'm not supposed to be playing on the riverbank anyway. Besides, I've never been in a boat like that. If it turned over, we might both drown."

I used the coffee can to bail out the water. I didn't figure Ernie was going to be much help with the boat.

A few days later I made it over to the island. It wasn't easy. The current was swift and the homemade paddle didn't work too well. I finally got to the upper end of the island and landed. When I stepped out, I sank down in the mud over my shoe tops. This wasn't too good, and I decided to wait until the weather got drier. I was also going to have a problem about my shoes and socks. I was in luck this time. Nobody was home when I got back and I managed to clean up pretty well. Next time I might not be as lucky. I would have to take a towel and come home clean. My mother knew I was a good swimmer, but she would have had an absolute fit if she found out that I owned a boat.

The next few days it rained a lot, and I didn't have a chance to check up on my boat. When I finally went down to see about it, the river was way up. The island was under water, and my boat was gone. The rope was still tied to the tree limb, and I hoped that the boat was on the other end of it. I would have to wait until the water went down, which would probably take a few days. I didn't live far from the river, so I checked every day. The water stayed up. I wondered if the island would wash away. So far the island had been a big disappointment to me. It wouldn't be much fun to have a hut if you had to wade in the mud to get to it. Maybe it would dry out when the weather got warmer. My rope was still tied to the tree limb, and I waited anxiously for the river to go down.

The river finally did go down, and the island was still there. My boat was still there, too, but sunk deeper in the mud. It was going to take some digging to get it out, and I was going to have to do it by myself.

I found a small shovel that my mother had used in the fireplace. It would have to do. I went back to the riverbank, took off my shoes and rolled up my pants. It was a mean, dirty job and took a while, but I got most of the mud shoveled out. The boat looked a little sad and was sitting about six or seven feet above the water. I gave it a shove, but there was no way I was going to get it back in the water without help. Ernie and Tom and finally Osgood came and looked at it, but none of them would help. It was pretty clear that I was going to have to have more help.

I had tried to solve my mud problem by keeping out an old pair of shoes and a towel, which I kept in a tree crotch near the boat. I wouldn't have passed close inspection, but I did manage to clean up a little bit before I went home. This worked all right as far as the mud was concerned, but it didn't help me get the boat back in the water.

Matt was the biggest boy in our class. He was not only overgrown, but had been held back for two years. He was man-size. After school I got him aside and said, ''Matt, I need some help. I'll give you fifty cents to help me put my boat back in the river.'' It was going to take my week's allowance, but it sounded like a good deal to him. When Matt saw the boat, he waded into the mud and shoved it right back into the water. I gave him the fifty cents, and he went home. I don't know how Matt explained being so muddy.

I had had about enough mud myself and decided that it was time to take the boat to the country club. The country club had a floating dock, and I figured I could tie the boat up there and stay relatively clean. It was going to be about a two-mile trip—maybe two-thirds of it on the Etowah and the other third on the Coosa. The Oostanaula River, which is a good bit bigger than the Etowah, joins the Etowah near downtown Rome and forms the Coosa. The Coosa is a good-size river. I would have about a half a mile on the Coosa before I got to the club.

Tom and Ernie came to see me off but declined to make the trip. They said they would meet me on the club dock and help me get it tied up. I shoved off and hoped for the best. The trip down the Etowah was not too bad. I managed to stay about in the middle of the river, but when I got to the Coosa, it was a different proposition. The Ostanaula came in swift and muddy, and I was out in the middle and pretty scared. I hadn't figured on the river looking so wide and the current being so swift, but there wasn't a whole lot I could do about it. I started paddling with the old home-made paddle but wasn't making much progress toward the bank. I had figured that getting to the club dock would not be too much of a problem, but I was wrong. Ernie and Tom were on the dock waving when I went by. I missed the landing by ten or twelve feet and went on downstream. Maybe a quarter of a mile further, I managed to grab the branches of an overhanging tree and pulled the boat into the bank. I was nervous and scared, but I was back on the bank. I tied the boat up pretty good to a tree and got out. I had no idea how I would get the boat back to the dock; certainly I couldn't paddle it back against the current with my home-made paddle. Maybe the current would slow down in a few days, but the paddle wasn't going to get any better. Ernie and Tom came down through the bushes, relieved to see me back on land. They hadn't been much help, but Ernie took me on the back of his bicycle, and we went on back to town.

15

I emptied my savings bank. I had a little over a dollar in change. I'd spent most of my money buying the boat, but I really needed a new paddle. I stopped by Owens Hardware and bought a new paddle which Mr. Owens let me have for a dollar. When I walked across the bridge, I thought the river was down a little and the current a little quieter. Maybe with the new paddle I would get the boat back to the dock. I was certainly going to try.

Deacon Coppedge, the club manager, was near the river bank talking to some of the caddies. He obviously was not pleased with their behavior. The Deacon could be pretty loud at times, but when he saw me he stopped talking to the caddies.

"Aren't you Mr. Magruder's boy?" he said.

"Yes, sir," I said.

"Are you the one that had that old boat tied up down back of number seven green?"

"Yes, sir. That's my boat."

"I'm sorry to tell you it *was* your boat. Yesterday a scrawny little man in a gray hat came by here, said his name was Billy Bob and that he was a friend of yours. Said he needed to borrow the boat bad, but he would bring it back to you in a few days. I doubt if he will. He smelled pretty strong of whiskey to me."

I doubted if he would either. I walked on down to number seven and looked where I had tied the boat up. It was gone. Maybe Billy Bob had decided it was time to really get away and was floating down the river toward Mobile. He was in my boat, but I don't guess he was worried about that. I put my new paddle on my shoulder and started walking toward town. I wondered if Mr. Owens would take the paddle back.

ૐ

The Rome news reported today that the body of a while male found below the dam at Mayo's Bar has been identified as that of Billy Bob Robinson of 305 East 6th Avenue. Authorities believe that Robinson was an occupant of a small boat that accidentally drifted over the dam. Robinson was formerly employed at the Lindale Mill as a loop fixer. He is survived by his wife, Bertha Mae. Funeral arrangements are incomplete and will be announced later.

Steamboating on the Coosa

My UNCLE GEORGE was captain of a steamboat. We've got his pilot's license, which authorized him to command steam-powered vessels on the Coosa-Alabama river system and its tributaries. He was eighteen years old when the license was issued. George went to work for Captain John Seay, the owner and operator of the White Star Steamship Lines. His first command, the *Resaca* was the oldest and smallest of the White Star's boats, but from time to time he commanded the larger and newer boats, including the *Clifford B. Seay* flagship of the line. For the larger boats, navigation on the Coosa was limited to the area from Rome to Greensport, just south of Gadsden, Alabama. From Greensport to Wetumptka, Alabama, a series of rapids made navigation impossible.

Nearly every farm had its own landing, and although cotton was the principal commodity, the boats carried all manner of cargo, including fertilizer, seed, poultry, farm animals, and passengers. The boats were also frequently chartered for parties and outings of various kinds—a picture of the *Resaca* shows a duck-hunting party on its return from a successful hunt on the river.

Competition was keen among the boats hauling cargo between Rome and Gadsden, particularly after the railroads were extended to north Georgia and northeast Alabama. There were occasional reports of hijacked cargo. It was a time of colorful characters, and Uncle George seems to have played his part. When the railroads finally put the steamboats out of business,

George became a banker and spent the rest of his life wearing nice clothes and looking very serious and doing a good job of worrying about other people's money.

≥▲

The *Resaca* had been to Gadsden, Alabama, carrying a miscellaneous cargo of poultry, eggs, seed, some fertilizer, and a few passengers. George sat in his captain's chair and turned the wheel over to his mate, Tim.

"If business doesn't get better, I'm going to have to look for another line of work. We didn't carry enough cargo to Gadsden to pay the hands, much less us. I'm still a young man, and I'm getting a little tired of steering this old tub up and down the river, particularly when it's mostly empty."

Tim narrowly missed the spittoon, but neither he nor George seemed to notice.

"Captain, I'm not a young man anymore, and I don't know any other line of work. I've been hanging around the rivers since I was a boy, and being mate on the *Resaca* is the best job I ever had. I'm too old to plow with a mule or pick cotton. Maybe Colonel Seay would give me a job around the dock, but if business doesn't get better, the Colonel may be looking for something himself."

George didn't seem to be listening.

"If the steamboat business plays out, I'd like to have a job where I'd wear good clothes and have an office. Oh, I can dress up occasionally and put on my captain's uniform and cap, but you know, Tim, most of the time it's hard to tell us from the hands, except we're white and they're black. Maybe I'll be a banker or an undertaker. I don't think the dead bodies would worry me too much, but I'd hate to fool with all the relatives. And then there's that business of looking sad and pious all the time. I don't think I'd like that. I like to smile and laugh a lot. I guess I won't be an undertaker, although they do seem to wear good clothes and make good money most of the time. My father was a soldier most of his life, but there is not any future in that now, and never was for that matter. He ended up being chief of police, which is probably the reason I spent all my time on the river to get away from home. He wasn't one to take much foolishness. I could be a banker; I've got a cousin who runs a bank, and he would probably give me a job. You do have to be serious-minded though. Since you're looking after other folks' money, they expect you to be serious about it. I would have to dress up in good clothes and go sit in an office all day—what do you think about it, Tim?''

Tim shut his eyes as if to concentrate better and missed the spittoon again.

"Damn, Tim. Why don't you spit out the window like everybody else? I'm going to throw that spittoon overboard, or take it home and use it for a flower pot.''

George manfully shifted the tobacco from one side of his jaw to the other and spat out of the wheelhouse.

"Captain, I doubt if that made it all the way to the river, maybe you ought to try the spittoon.''

"Damn, Tim. Do you think I'm old enough to quit chewing tobacco? I never did like the stuff, but all the other captains chew it or smoke cigars. I don't think I could grow a real good beard, and a thin one would be worse than nothing. I would like to get rid of this chewing tobacco, though.''

"Captain, with all due respect, I don't think you look old enough to quit chewing tobacco yet. You gonna have to go on chewing for a while yet.''

The *Resaca* rounded the point of Morton's Bend.

"Tim, look at Morton's landing and tell me what you see.''

"Lord, Lord, Captain. There must be two hundred bales of cotton sittin' on that landing waiting to be hauled somewhere. I'll bet they're waiting on the *Magnolia* and won't let us have a bale.''

George took the wheel and headed in toward the landing.

"As soon as we get the boards down, you and the boys start loading cotton. I'll do all the talking. You just do the loading and let me handle it."

The boards went down and Tim and the boys started loading cotton.

A distinguished-looking elderly black man walked up and began to remonstrate.

"Captain, don't take any of that cotton—that cotton's spoken for. Mr. Morton told me he'd made special arrangements with Captain Coulter, and the *Magnolia* is on the way to carry all this cotton to Rome. Don't take it, Captain. There'll be trouble, sure."

"Why, John, you know me. You know the old *Resaca* will carry this cotton high and dry and deliver it straight in to Mr. Shropshire's warehouse."

"Captain, that's another thing. Mr. Morton don't like Shropshire, and he particularly said he didn't want Shropshire having anything to do with his cotton. He and Captain Coulter's got some sort of special arrangements about this load. Please, Captain, tell those boys to quit loading and leave this cotton alone."

The cotton was fast disappearing from the landing while George and John carried on a long and heated conversation.

"Captain, I can't stop you, but I'm telling you not to take that cotton. There's going to be bad trouble. I'm a lone man, and I've

done all I can do. The *Magnolia* is on her way, and I'll have to tell Mr. Morton and Captain Coulter what happened.''

''I'm sure they won't blame you, John, but tell Mr. Morton that the cotton is going to be safe and sound and the receipts will be at the White Star office.''

There was one bale of cotton left on the landing. Tim looked at it and shook his head.

''Captain, the old *Resaca* is too full now—we can't take on another bale. I'm afraid when we get back on she may roll over. Like it is, I don't know how we'll get past Mayo's Bar.''

''You may be right, Tim, and it's sort of insulting to Captain Coulter to leave one bale of cotton for a big fine ship like the *Magnolia*. Why don't we put off another bale so things will look better?''

George gave a long blast on the *Resaca's* whistle and the *Resaca* started toward Rome.

''Captain, those two bales look a little lonesome, and I think old John is going to give us a lot of trouble. He was awful upset about us taking the cotton.''

''Tim, we're not stealing this cotton. We are a commercial cargo vessel, duly licensed to haul cotton on this river. We are going to deposit this cotton at the landing and tell the dray people to take it to the warehouse. I will then personally take the papers and leave them for Mr. Morton at the White Star Line office. Everything will be very regular, and if anything should happen, I'm the captain, and I told you to do it.''

The old *Resaca* was overloaded and made slow progress, but was not far from Rome when the *Magnolia* passed. She was empty and obviously expecting a cargo. The boats gave the customary courtesy salutes as they passed each other. The *Magnolia's* mate was handling the wheel.

''Captain, where do you think George Magruder got all that cotton?'' The captain's face was grim.

''I don't know where he got it, but it better not have been at Morton's landing.''

22

The cotton was duly deposited in Mr. Shropshire's warehouse and the paperwork on Captain Seay's desk. George was happy with his day's work, but thought it prudent not to await the *Magnolia*'s return.

George and his mother were having supper when Captain Seay knocked on the door. George answered it and, seeing his employer, stepped out on the porch. Captain Seay, the owner of the White Star Steamship Line, had given George his first job and the men were fast friends, despite a considerable difference in their ages.

"George, I'm afraid we've got trouble. Morton and the Negro, John Barton, came to Rome on the *Magnolia*. John Barton says that you took that cotton by force, over his objections, and that you threatened him with bodily harm if he tried to interfere. Captain Coulter is a fair man, and I have never seen him so mad. They have just left my office on the way to see lawyer Featherston. I don't know what he'll tell them, but they plan to do something if they can. You and I are good friends, but you are still young and made a mistake in taking that cotton. I don't want the White Star Line involved in any lawsuits, and I don't think you do either. You need to go talk to Captain Coulter, and I don't think you had better wait too long."

"John, I'll do anything you say. I don't want to hurt the line. I do hate like hell to apologize to the old bastard—he thinks he owns the river now. I don't see how he could really do much. I brought that cotton back to Rome and put it in the warehouse. He's not really out anything but his commission."

"I know, George, but you don't have any idea how mad those people were. They already think you are a smart-ass young guy who needs to be taken down, and they are fixing to do it if they can."

"John, don't worry about it. I'll go see Coulter in the morning."

"Fine, George. But don't wait too long."

George spent an uneasy night. He was beginning to regret

taking the cotton, although he couldn't see that it was such a serious thing, for he had delivered every bale to the warehouse and left all the receipts for Mr. Morton. Maybe he ought to go see Coulter. He certainly didn't want to get John Seay in any trouble.

George was still dressing when there was a heavy knock on the door. His mother opened the door to his bedroom. She looked upset.

"George, are you in any trouble? Sheriff Horton is in the parlor waiting to see you. I asked him in for coffee, but he said he needed to see you as soon as possible."

The sheriff was a big man and no longer young. George had known him for a long time.

"George, you had better sit down. I've got real bad news for you."

The sheriff pulled a legal-looking document out of his pocket. "This is a warrant for your arrest on a charge of piracy. I never had one of these before, but lawyer Featherston fixed it up for Mr. Morton and Captain Coulter. He says I'm supposed to arrest you and hold you in the county jail for the federal authorities. I served under your father in the war and under him in the police department; there was never a finer man in the world, and I don't want to put his son in my jail. I may get in trouble, but I'll hold this thing up, at least until tomorrow morning. But in the meantime, you had better get yourself a lawyer and figure out what you're going to do."

George didn't go to see Captain Coulter, he went to the White Star office and told John Seay what was happening. Seay was upset.

"George, we had better get you a lawyer right now."

Judge Meyhart did not keep them waiting.

"George, I've already heard about the warrant. I figured John would want me to help you if I can, and I have been looking at the federal statutes. I've never had occasion to look it up before, but it's really pretty simple. Piracy consists of taking the goods

24

of another without the owner's consent and transporting them on a vessel on the navigable waterways of the United States or its tributaries. Theft is not involved, only the unlawful taking and transportation on navigable waters. John tells me that you did pick up the cotton over the objection of the Negro John Barton. You may be guilty even though the cotton is in the warehouse.''

George was still smiling. He turned to Colonel Meyhart.

''Colonel, I understand what you read, and I guess maybe I'm guilty of that, but I didn't steal the cotton. What can they do to you for that? The only thing that happened was that Captain Coulter didn't get his commission and maybe Mr. Morton wanted his cotton in a different warehouse, but that doesn't seem to be so bad.''

Colonel Meyhart did not smile.

''George, you had better sit back down and let me read the rest of this statute. I now read to you from Section 32-15 sub (b) of the Federal Penal Code. 'Piracy is hereby declared to be a capital felony. A person convicted under the foregoing sections of the code shall be subject to a maximum punishment of hanging by the neck until pronounced dead.' ''

Colonel Meyhart looked up.

''Do you want me to read any more, George?''

George had turned pale and, at least for the moment, was unable to say anything.

''George, I don't think they're going to hang you, but this is a serious matter, and you can be put to an enormous amount of trouble and embarrassment. Under our judicial system, a person is ordinarily entitled to bail or bond. However, in the case of a capital felony, the accused has no absolute right to bail, which can only be granted by a federal judge. Unless this matter is settled, Sheriff Horton will have no alternative except to lock you up in his jail and hold you until the U.S. Marshall comes from Atlanta. The marshal can either hold you in the local jail or take you to Atlanta. The judge in Atlanta can grant bail or he can order you confined until trial. The case would be tried in Rome, and Judge Ferguson won't be in Rome to hold court for another three months. Even if a jury finds you innocent, it's possible that you would have spent three months or more in jail. As far as I know, you are a fine young man who has made an error in judgment. John Seay says that you are a fine river pilot, and he will help you if he can. A good bit of what is going to happen depends entirely on you.''

George had recovered his power of speech, but not his composure.

''For God's sake, Colonel, you're my lawyer, or I hope you are—tell me what to do. I don't want to be locked up in the county jail, much less hung.''

''George, I know Mr. Morton and Captain Coulter very well. They are fine, honorable men, but they are both mad as hell at you, and lawyer Featherston is telling them what to do. I want you to walk out of here, take your captain's hat in your hand and go down to see Captain Coulter. Tell him that you were wrong, that you know you were wrong, that you are young and have made a bad error in judgment, and that you are willing to do anything that he wants you to do. He will probably want you to pay his expenses, including the *Magnolia*'s trip to Morton's Bend, and any other expenses he's incurred. Maybe John Seay will lend you some money or maybe Coulter will let you sign a note, but my advice is to do whatever they tell you to do and get rid of that warrant. I'll be here all afternoon. You might let me know what happens. If I have to, I'll go to see Coulter and Morton myself and talk to Featherston.''

Captain Coulter was in his office, but seemed in no hurry to see George, who waited because there was nothing else he could do. Finally, Captain Coulter opened the door, looked coldly at George, and said, ''What are you doing here? I thought you were in jail.''

''Captain, I've got my hat in my hand, and I'll get down on my knees if I have to. I need to talk with you.''

''Well, if that's the way it is, come on in and shut the door.''

26

Captain Coulter sat behind his big desk and let George stand. "I was wrong, Captain Coulter. I've made a bad mistake. I want to apologize and do anything I can to make up for it."

"You seem to have undergone a considerable change since yesterday. I was told that when you brought my cotton to the landing, you were bragging about beating the *Magnolia* to it and laughing about leaving two bales for the *Magnolia* to pick up. I'm not sure that I can do anything about the federal warrant. It may be that the matter will just have to take its normal course, but if I can take it up, I will certainly expect you to pay our expenses in full—my commission, the cost of sending the *Magnolia* down to Morton's Bend, Mr. Morton's expenses in making an unplanned trip to Rome, and also lawyer Featherston's fee."

"You're right, Captain Coulter, and I'm willing to pay, but I don't have any money right now. You know things have been slow on the river, but I will certainly pay as soon as I can."

"You'll have to do some better than that. Lawyer Featherston has fixed up a ninety-day note for the entire amount, plus ten percent interest. If you want to sign this note and tell John Seay to start taking the money out of your paychecks, I'll see what I can do about the warrant."

George signed and pushed the note back to Captain Coulter.

"You seem to be a little nervous this morning, George, but that's not all bad. Men need to be nervous occasionally, particularly young, smart men."

George sat in Captain Seay's office and looked down at the floor. "I did what Colonel Meyhart told me to. I signed my life away. I didn't have anything anyway, but now I've got less than anything. I guess it's a good thing lawyer Featherston didn't know I had my father's gold watch and cufflinks, or they would have gotten them too. If you want me to leave, I will. Maybe my cousin Sproull will give me a job at his bank."

"Quit carrying on, George, and put your captain's hat back on your head. You're the best pilot I've got, and the railroads haven't killed us yet. I think we're going to have a few more

27

years of good steamboating, but we've got to work hard. By the way, Captain Benjamin isn't feeling well today, and I want you to take the *Clifford B. Seay* to Gadsden. There is some late cotton coming in, and we've got lots of promises about cargo. You could be gone two or three days and make a good bit of money—part of which I will have to give to Captain Coulter. Are you ready to go or not?''

George stood up, put his Captain's cap back on and managed a smile.

''I'm ready, sir. Can you send word to my mother that everything is going to be all right and that I will be back as soon as I can? And, John, can I take Tim as mate?''

''I don't know what you want with him. I know one thing, he'd better not mess up Captain Benjamin's wheelhouse. The Captain keeps all the woodwork polished, including the hardwood floor.''

''I'd like to take Tim. We are old friends and it can get sort of lonesome in the wheelhouse. I'll make him put some newspapers under his spittoon—after all, anybody can make a mistake occasionally.''

The *Clifford B. Seay* pulled into the landing at Coosa. There was a good bit of cargo on the landing, including some cotton and other produce.

''Tim, go see what we got and be damn sure it isn't spoken for. I'm not sure whether I'm on probation or not, but I can't take the chance. Who is that nice-looking woman standing over there with those packages? She doesn't look like a passenger.''

''That's the widow Barlow. She lives down here somewhere and is a special friend of Captain Coulter. I thought you might know her.''

''I don't, but I guess I ought to see what she wants. After all, I owe the old bastard a lot of money.''

George took off his cap and smiled brightly. The widow was a nice-looking lady, well dressed, maybe a little past middle-age.

''My, you are young for a captain. I was hoping that Captain Coulter would come down.''

"Sorry, ma'am, but the *Magnolia* is undergoing repairs, and I doubt if Captain Coulter will be down for a while."

"Well, he is a close friend of our family, and tomorrow is his birthday. I've knitted him a little something for the cold weather and also baked him a birthday cake. I wonder if you would be good enough to take it to him for me?"

"The present we can take all right, but we're on the way to Greensport and I'm not sure how well the cake would travel."

"Oh, well. It's already baked, so do the best you can." She smiled. "If the trip takes too long, maybe you and your mate will have to eat it and tell the captain how good it was."

"We'll do our best, ma'am. I'm sure the captain will be sorry that he wasn't able to take the presents personally."

Captain Seay had promised them a good trip and they picked up and discharged a good bit of cargo.

"Tim, I think we might even make a little money this trip, although I don't get to keep much of it. I don't want Captain Coulter to revoke my probation or call my note, but I've got a feeling that cake is not going to make it all the way to Greensport and back. What do you think, Tim? If we decide that it's not going to make the whole trip, it would be silly to wait until it gets stale."

"In some ways, Captain, you are a smart man. That cake looks like it's getting a little crumbly to me. Why don't we check on it?"

"Tim, the widow Barlow is an excellent cook as well as a nice-looking lady. We will certainly deliver the sweater, or whatever it is, but after all, the captain of a cargo ship is the sole judge of when perishable cargo has perished."

The *Clifford B. Seay*, having completed a successful trip to Greensport, Alabama, tied up at the landing at the foot of Myrtle Hill. George picked up the birthday package. "Tim, I think you had better go with me. I can explain to Captain Coulter how, in a fit of hunger, you ate his birthday cake."

"For God's sake, Captain, don't say anything like that. I'm

taking a big enough risk sailing as your mate without adding anything to it.''

George carried the package when they knocked on Captain Coulter's office door. He seemed surprised to see them, and didn't suggest that they sit down. ''Well, George, what can I do for you?''

''Tim and I have just gotten back from Greensport, and on the way down we stopped off at Coosa. We want to wish you a happy birthday on behalf of the widow Barlow and to deliver the present that she entrusted to us.''

Captain Coulter looked pleased and opened the package, which turned out to be a heavy red wool sweater. He smiled. ''At least they will be able to see me coming. She's a fine woman and has had a hard time since Harry died. Why don't you both sit down. I was just making a cup of coffee.''

George and Tim sat on the edge of their chairs and waited for events to develop. Captain Coulter continued his observations.

''Harry and Melinda lived near the Coosa landing and I often went up for a meal and sometimes spent the night. She is a very fine cook.''

George shifted uneasily on the edge of his chair. ''Well, we need to tell you about that. She also baked you a nice cake with ''Happy Birthday'' written on it, but we've been on a long trip and the cake didn't travel very well. We had to consider it perishable cargo.''

Now Captain Coulter was smiling broadly. ''You mean you ate my birthday cake? I know it was good and I hope you enjoyed it. Fortunately, I have another cake, which I have not quite finished.'' He opened a cabinet at the back of his desk and produced a half-eaten cake. ''I know I'll enjoy the sweater, and I know how it is with perishable cargo. I hope you boys will have a slice of cake with your coffee.''

Queen of the Ferry

"'Drop that thing overboard! Right now!'"

"Gee, Daddy. We just got it going."

"Dammit, Billy! I said drop it over! Don't you see that game warden's boat coming down the river?"

The thing, with wires attached, disappeared into the muddy waters of the Coosa.

"Sandra, get in the water and sort of swim around. See if you can keep an eye on where we dropped it. I'm not sure whether being under water is going to hurt it or not, but it belongs to Cousin Robert, and he probably wants it back."

Sandra jumped overboard and began to tread water as the game wardens approached in their small outboard.

Sandra's daddy, Lee Allgood, hailed the officers as they came up.

"Why, Clyde Angle. I didn't know you had gone in the game warden business."

"I ain't been in it very long, Lee. In fact, this is my first assignment. The boys in Montgomery finally got excited about this fish-shocking business and passed two or three new laws about it. We're supposed to be looking for these things, although I don't think I ever really saw one, except hanging on the wall. But the captain said to me, 'Clyde, you know Lee Allgood. He's been down there on the river running Garrett's Ferry for a long time. He probably knows whether anybody is shocking fish or not. Why don't you go down there and talk to him?'

"I told the captain you and me had been buddies for a long time and that if anybody was shocking fish, it was probably you. Captain said, 'Well, buddies or not, if he's shocking fish, you arrest him and bring him in. They told us to stop fish shocking in Cherokee County, although I can't rightly say it got started up here.'

"Lee, you know this stretch of river better than anybody in the county. You know anything about all this fish shocking? I'd like to arrest somebody, seeing as this is my first assignment."

"Clyde, I'd like to help you, but I'm not even sure how the thing works. 'Course, everybody's heard about it. They tell me it has been against the law in Georgia for a long time. I don't know why the boys in Montgomery finally got excited about it. How does it work anyway?"

"Well, the way I understand it, you take an old crank telephone and put the wires on either side of the boat and let them dangle in the water. Then you crank on that phone, and they tell me it puts out an awful shock that sort of numbs the fish so that they float up to the top, and you just pick them up. Seems a little unfair to the fish, but I understand it works mostly on catfish, and I think we've got plenty of them. What you folks doing out in the boat? I don't see any fishing poles."

"We don't use poles very much, Clyde. It's too slow, and we need to eat. We're going to work a couple of our trot lines and check a few limb hooks to see if we got anything for supper. Next time you are down this way, why don't you stop in at the ferry house and visit a little? Somedays it's pretty slow."

Sandra climbed out and sat on the riverbank trying to keep her eyes focused on the spot where the old telephone had disappeared.

"Daddy, I think it's right down there, but I've been looking at that water so long I can't be a hundred percent sure. If those game wardens are gone, I can dive down and try to find it."

"I guess we'd better wait a little while. I don't think it would look too great for a ferry man to get arrested for shocking catfish—particularly after they were asking me for help. When we find it, I'm going to call Robert and tell him to come and get it. I don't think a few catfish are worth a fine."

⁊⦁

The Coosa River snakes back and forth across the farmlands in northeast Alabama. It's a wide, deep river, and there used to be a lot of ferries. My daddy ran Garrett's Ferry, when it was the only good way for the folks in Pollard's Bend to get to town. They could go down to Leesburg and cross the bridge there, but that was a long way around to Centre, which is the county seat. There is a lot of good farming land in Pollard's Bend, and we had a good bit of traffic most of the time. It was a county ferry, and we didn't have to run at night, but during the daylight we

had to run back and forth as long as people wanted to get across the river. You may have seen one of those ferries, although I don't think there are but one or two left. Our boat would hold two cars at a time and a good many people if they had been walking. The boat was attached to a cable that ran across the river. I'm not sure I ever understood exactly how it worked, but Daddy would crank a windless on the boat that would change the angle of the boat to the current, and depending on the angle, the boat would go back and forth across the river powered by the current. It didn't have any motor, just the angle of the boat and the river current. It worked pretty well, but sometime when the river got up real high, we had to tie the boat to the bank and tell folks they had to go to Leesburg or stay at home. My daddy ran the ferry mostly, but sometimes my mama had to go down and run it with Billy and me helping. Billy and I could run it by ourselves, and we did a few times, but we weren't supposed to because neither of us was old enough.

We knew most of the people who used the ferry. Some of them went back and forth every day to work in Centre. Our favorite was Dr. Ambrose Poovey, a medical doctor. He made house calls and had a lot of patients in Pollard's Bend. He loved to hunt, and would shoot at practically anything—not only birds, but rabbits, squirrels, snakes, and anything else he happened to see. He went on trips to shoot at things. I loved to hear him tell about some of his trips. He had been to the Rocky Mountains, and even made two trips to Africa. He promised to take me to see his trophies, but he never did. He always got out of the car and talked with us while we were crossing the river. He would pat me on the head, and I remember one day he said, "Lee, this is a pretty little girl you've got. Why don't you make her quit running this ferry and let her go to school like she ought to? She could probably be homecoming queen over there at Centre High School."

"Now, Doc, you know that Sandra goes to a school every day. It's not but a mile from the ferry to the school. I wouldn't keep her out to help me run this ferry, although she's strong and good help when she wants to be. I don't think she's ever going to be homecoming queen, though; she's too skinny."

"Well, she is a little thin, but she'll probably fill out some. She's a pretty thing, though, and I never really cared much for fat girls. The next time I go off hunting, I'm going to bring her back a present—maybe like some buffalo horns or something she could hang on the wall."

I liked Dr. Poovey and I liked what he said about me being pretty. Maybe if I ate a little more and didn't swim so much, I could be homecoming queen. I didn't care much about the buffalo horns, though, and would just as soon he bring me something else.

We didn't see Dr. Poovey for a while. Somebody said he was out west hunting wild goats, and the doctor that was taking his place didn't make house calls. Finally one day Dr. Poovey showed up again in a brand new four-door automobile. He was on his way to Pollard's Bend and I guess was going to shoot at something on the way, because I saw his old shotgun on the back seat. He drove the new car onto the ferry, and he and Billy got to talking about cars. It was drizzling a little, and Billy put up all the windows—maybe that was the reason he didn't get the chain down tight on the car—and about halfway across the river, I noticed the doctor's car was moving backwards and that the gate wasn't chained up. We had some walking passengers on board and everybody started hollering at once. The hollering didn't do Doc's car any good though; it slipped on backwards and off the ferry.

People will tell you that an automobile can't float, but Dr. Poovey's car had a lot of room inside and the windows were up. It bobbed up and down a little and started down the river. Daddy hollered for Billy and me to chase it, and we jumped in the bateau and started after it. It wasn't moving very fast and seemed to be sinking a little lower in the water. Billy got a rope around the rear bumper, which was beginning to stick up, but there wasn't much he could do with it. Daddy and all the people on the ferry were hollering instructions. Billy gave me the end of the rope and told me to tie it to a tree. I jumped in and swam to the bank, and pretty soon we had the doctor's car anchored to a tree, but it kept sinking, and soon it had sunk as far as it was going to and ended up with the rear bumper sticking up out of the water. I was cold and wet and walked on back up to the house to get dried off.

Afterwards, Daddy told me that Dr. Poovey said that he wasn't much worried about the car because he had plenty of insurance, but that he hated losing his Parker double-barrel shotgun and that if somebody could get it out of the car, he would really appreciate it. So the next day Billy and I dove down and tried to open the car door, but it was jammed on something and we couldn't get in. The car didn't look like it was going anywhere, so we figured we would get the gun out sometime, although it might be pretty rusted up by then.

Maybe about a week later a man came to the ferry house. He said he was an insurance adjuster and had come to look at Dr.

Poovey's car. I took him down to the river and showed him the rear bumper sticking up out of the water. He sort of shook his head and wrote a few things down in a little book he had. I figured he would probably be back—maybe the insurance company would try to pull the car out, but it was in a bad place and the bank was awful steep.

One day when I got home from school, my mama was sitting in the rocking chair on the porch reading some papers.

"Sandra, you'd better look at these things. I can't read too well with my new glasses, and we need to be sure that everything is legal. The insurance man sold Dr. Poovey's car to Billy for ten dollars, and these are the settlement papers. Billy has already paid him the ten dollars and is probably down looking at his car—or what he can see of it."

The papers looked all right to me. Dr. Poovey had signed one turning the car over to the insurance company, and the company had signed another one turning it over to Billy. Billy really

37

wasn't old enough to own a car, but I figured that since the car wasn't going anywhere, it didn't matter.

I ran down to the river to see if anything was happening, and there sat Billy looking at the rear bumper of his car, which was still sticking out of the water and looked about the same to me.

"What are you going to do with that car?" I said.

"I don't know, but it must be worth something. I ought to be able to get ten dollars worth of parts off it, and maybe I can get inside and find the Doc's shotgun. If it's not too bad, I know he'll give me a reward for it."

It was a long, hot summer and the river got pretty low. We did a lot of swimming around Billy's automobile, and he must have got twenty-five or thirty dollars worth of parts off of it. One day a floating log went through the back window and Billy finally got Dr. Poovey's shotgun. It didn't look too bad to me, except it had some rust spots. Daddy and Billy soaked it with oil and got it to looking pretty good. Daddy said, "I think the Doc can get somebody to work on this thing and it'll be almost good as new. Why don't you kids go to town and take it by his office. It's a fine old shotgun, and I'm sure the doctor will appreciate getting it back."

Mama wrapped the shotgun up in some old Christmas paper, and Billy and I walked to town to deliver it to Dr. Poovey. His nurse said he was out making house calls in the other end of the county, and we had to leave the gun with her. I know Billy was disappointed because he was looking to get some sort of reward. The nurse was nice. She said, "I know Dr. Poovey will appreciate this, and he'll be seeing you young folks in a few days."

She was right. He drove on board the ferry and shook hands with Daddy and Billy. He gave Billy something, which I figured was a reward for the gun, and then turned to me. "You're getting prettier every day," he said. "Don't go off with the first one of these country boys that asks you. I got to thinking about those buffalo horns and decided that they really wouldn't make a very good present for a young lady. I have brought you something

38

else, though.'' He got out a pretty big package wrapped up in red paper.

"I hope you like it. Your cousin Lon over at the bait shop, helped me pick it out."

I didn't open it right then because I was on my way home and there were lots of folks on the ferry I didn't care about seeing my present. I wasn't all that sure myself. I didn't know much about Cousin Lon's taste, but I figured it wasn't a silk nightgown.

It was a pretty heavy package. I carried it home, shut the door, and pulled off the wrapping. The silver glinted in the sunlight from the window. A heavy silver picture frame. It must have cost a lot of money. Dr. Poovey smiled out in his most reassuring manner. He was wearing his hunting jacket and had his Parker double-barrel across his arm. In the corner, he had written, ''To the prettiest little girl in Cherokee County—Ambrose Poovey, M.D.''

My mama opened the door and picked up the picture. ''I'll bet it's solid silver and worth a lot of money. We'll have to put him in the living room for now. He'll probably come by to check.''

I sat it on the living room table and looked at it again. It was a nice frame, and Dr. Poovey looked pretty good for an older man.

Sailing with Ernie

Ernie said he knew how to sail, that he had taken a course in sailing at summer camp and remembered most of everything they taught him—besides, he had been sailing once or twice since then with his father-in-law, and in general thought that we would make out fine. Ernie's father-in-law, a doctor from Boston, owned a nice summer home on Cape Cod near Chatham. Ernie and his wife, Shirley, had made arrangements for us to stay in a neighbor's house, the neighbor having moved out to a garage apartment so that he could rent his home to tourists during the summer. I thought this a little unusual, but it was a nice house, and the owner seemed comfortable out in the apartment.

I was anxious to go sailing, so that afternoon Ernie and I went to look for a sailboat. We found a couple of small boats that were available for day sailing—one had one sail, and one had two sails. "I vote for the one with one sail," I told Ernie. "It's got to be simpler than two sails." The owner explained that it was a cat boat called *Wood Pussy* fifteen feet long, comfortable and easy to sail. We made arrangements to go out the next day, and paid a deposit.

Early the next morning we were off, loaded with fishing gear, sandwiches, ice, and other equipment. The sails were already on the boat, and since it had no motor, there wasn't much to do except to get aboard with our gear. The owner added life jackets and a paddle, and we were ready. There was a nice breeze blowing down the channel, and I assumed that that was where we were going. Ernie took the tiller, and I pulled up the sail. We were off all right, headed directly across the channel, and Ernie held to a steady course. In about ten minutes we ran directly into the opposite bank and stuck firmly in the mud and marsh grass.

"Don't worry. It'll come back to me all right," Ernie said.

"I hope so," I said, "but in the meantime, I'm going to have to go out and wade in that mud." I got out, sank halfway to my knees, grabbed the bow of the boat, and asked Ernie which way he wanted to go. I didn't want to hurt his feelings, but I felt that this was a good time to set our course.

"We want to go down the channel," he said.

I dragged the bow around and we were off again, this time heading down the middle of the channel toward the Atlantic Ocean.

I noticed that we seemed to be going pretty fast, and we concluded that not only was the wind behind us but that the tide was going out at a fast rate. We passed what appeared to be the last channel marker, and headed in the general direction of Gibraltar.

"Ernie, just how do we plan to get back to Chatham? That one paddle is not going to do us a lot of good out here."

Ernie appeared to be philosophical about our situation and remarked that he had been out of the Chatham inlet before and that the tide would certainly change and carry us back to the dock. I thought this was unusually optimistic, but it was a fine day.

Before long, we saw an object ahead of us that appeared to be a navigational aid of some kind. Ernie said, "That must be the sea buoy. I have read about these things, and I am sure that the outer limits of the channel are marked by a sea buoy, and that must be it."

"Well, you head for that thing," I said, "and I am going to try to hang on to it and hold what we've got."

"We're not supposed to do that," he said, "but under the circumstances, see what you can do." The current had slowed somewhat, and I grabbed onto the buoy as we went by. I managed to tie on our bow line, and our progress toward Spain was halted.

There was no reason not to, so we got out our fishing tackle, and before long Ernie had landed a strange fish that had wings. Ernie declared that it was not a flying fish, but a sea robin, and that they were good to eat. I like fish, almost any kind of fish, but I decided that I would pass on sea robins. We caught a lot of sea robins. In fact, we caught so many we began to throw them back and finally decided that we really didn't want any at all. I have never seen a sea robin in the fish market, so they must not be in any great demand.

True to Ernie's prediction, the tide began to turn, and before long we let go of the sea buoy and headed back toward Chatham. By the time we got to the channel entrance we were actually learning to sail a little bit with the help of a pretty strong incoming tide. We would go from one side of the channel to the other, making a little progress on each maneuver. Ernie explained that this operation was called ''tacking,'' and that even though the wind was against us, we would tack up the channel and, with the aid of the tide, eventually get back to the dock.

This was fun, and as we gained confidence, we tacked back and forth thinking that there really wasn't much to sailing after all.

We gained so much confidence that we sailed right past the sailboat dock and up the channel and into the main harbor of Chatham. The harbor was crowded with boats—anchored boats, boats at docks and boats on moorings. I am sure there must have been room for us to turn around in an acceptable manner, but Ernie headed straight for a large sailboat that was anchored in the harbor. We hit the big boat about amidships, and I remember the loud boom it made, like hitting a bass drum. There was no one aboard, and I grabbed the rail and got us turned around. "I don't think we hurt anything, but I think it's time for us to go back." If anyone saw us, they did not give chase; so, having gotten turned around, we headed back down the channel toward our dock.

The wind was now behind us and we made good progress even though the tide was coming in. No more tacking, just straight down the channel and we would soon be safely back. The owner was standing on the dock as we approached. I asked Ernie if he had any plans about docking, and he said he hadn't, that frankly he didn't remember this part of the sailing course. We headed straight for the dock, and I remember thinking that it was going to be a pretty hard landing. The owner probably thought so too, because when we were within about ten feet of the end of the dock, he jumped into the water, grabbed the bow of our boat and diverted it from a direct hit. Actually, we didn't hit the dock too hard, and it didn't hurt the boat a bit.

We paid for the fish bait, thanked the owner and left. He didn't say anything at all—just tied the boat up, looked to see if there was any damage to the bow, and took our bait money. He didn't seem to be mad, but he didn't say anything, not even "Have a nice day."

Back at the house, we mixed drinks and sat on the porch. Shirley asked us about the sail, and I told her it was great, that maybe we would go again before we had to go home. "Ernie," I said, "I don't think we did too bad. We got back all right and didn't hurt the boat. Maybe I should call and reserve the boat for day after tomorrow."

Ernie said, "I would prefer that you make the arrangements. Let me know what he says."

I went to the telephone and had a short conversation with the owner. "What did he say?" Ernie asked. "He didn't say very much, but all of his boats are booked up for the next month. He said that maybe we should try a place in Wellfleet."

Airborne

B.C. III STOOD NAKED in front of his full-length mirror. Turning sideways, he sucked in his stomach and examined his profile. He was flexing his biceps when Matt came out of the shower. "Still in love, I see—you're having quite an affair."

B.C. said something like "Huh," and Matt continued his observations.

"All that iron-pumping you've been doing has built up some nice muscles, but you ought not to get so carried away with yourself. Sometimes you scare me. I don't suppose you remember anything about Greek mythology, but there is some precedent for falling in love with yourself. You ought to read the story."

"Well, what was it? I know you're going to show off and tell me anyway. I'm not sure why I put up with such a smart-ass roommate. Go ahead. Tell me the story."

"Well, there was this character named Narcissus, who was wandering around in the woods one day and happened to lean over a pool of water and see his own reflection. He was a good-looking young fellow and immediately fell in love with himself. Unfortunately, he tried to give himself a kiss, fell in the water, and drowned."

"That's a hell of a story. Is there supposed to be some moral in it? I think I look pretty good, maybe if you'd pump a little iron you wouldn't be embarrassed to put on your swimming trunks. Women like strong, good-looking men."

"Okay, B.C. Let's not argue about it. You are a strong, good-

looking young man even if you are not very smart. We are going to have a great weekend in the mountains. I talked to my father last night, and he is going to let us use the lake cabin and even his new motorboat. He loves that motorboat, so nothing better happen to it. I don't think we've got any water skis yet, but the lake is a little narrow for skiing anyway. We can go up and down at full speed and shake up all of our neighbors, who will probably be sitting on their docks.''

B.C. III looked at himself with approval. ''I'm ready. What do we do about women?''

''Women are absolutely no problem. There are at least three girls' camps on the mountain, and each one of them is run by a covey of college girls brought in especially to mind the little ones and to teach them basket-weaving and other skills. I don't think they have ugly counselors, although there may be a few borderline cases. My mother is a good friend of the woman that runs Camp Desoto. She'll pick us out a couple of nice-looking ones. If we don't like them, we can swap them in and she'll pick us out some different ones. There is a problem, though. These girls have to get back by 10:30, so there won't be any all-night stuff. You will have to exert your charms in the afternoon or early evening.''

''Matt, I've got to go on to class and won't be back until this afternoon. I'll come on up tomorrow morning, so if you leave this afternoon, write a note and tell me how to find the place.''

''It's pretty easy, and I am going on up after a while. I'll pick up some groceries, and you can bring the beer. If you get lost, call Camp Desoto and they'll direct you.''

≀▲

A good many years ago some Yankee developers decided that Lookout Mountain would be a great place to build a lake, golf course, and what are now called "other amenities." They bought about a thousand acres near Cloudland, Georgia, and built a dam across the east fork of Little River. Little River is really a creek, but it generally manages to keep the lake full. The dam is concrete and nearly fifty feet high. When there is a reasonable amount of rainfall, the water runs over the dam and under the roadway, which is separated from the top of the dam by some concrete arches. The arches may be eight or nine feet wide and another eight or nine feet high. Below the dam, Little River tries to get itself back together, and there are generally some sizable puddles.

The hotel got started but was never finished; the golf course was built but later grew up in grass and trees. That left the lake, and at the foreclosure sale a good many local people bought lots, so that there is now a modest cottage colony scattered along the lakeshore.

I don't know who named the lake "Lahoosage," but that's what it's called. In northwest Georgia and northeast Alabama we have an embarrassing habit of using what we think are Cherokee Indian names. After the way we treated the Cherokees, we ought to be too embarrassed to mention them; but apparently we're not, although the names probably aren't real Cherokee names anyway.

Lahoosage is a nice mountain lake—sort of Y-shaped, with the long side wandering maybe two miles from where the creek comes in to the dam. It's generally clear and cold and pretty nice except for the motor boats. The residents should have banned motorboats years ago, but they didn't, and now on a weekend afternoon they roar up and down making waves and noise. Some people even water-ski, although when you get to the dam you have to slow down so that the skier sinks and has to get back up for the return trip. Most everybody seems to have a good time, and I think there has been only one serious accident.

≥

Matt already had the girls when B.C. arrived. One was a little chubby, and Matt assigned her to B.C., who accepted the assignment without protest and thought that maybe he would not have to swap her in.

The new boat was on a trailer behind the house. Matt hadn't had a chance to try it out, but his dad said it would do forty miles an hour, which would get you to the dam and back pretty fast. There was no particular hurry about putting it in, so they all went swimming and sat around on the dock. The boys had a couple of beers, but the girls were afraid to join them because they had to go back to camp. B.C. was impressive with his muscles, and Matt thought that he was secretly tensing them to enhance the effect. Matt thought he looked pretty good himself, but decided that pumping a little iron probably wouldn't hurt. He soon found that he had met his date before—she was a slim, pretty brunette named Debby, and he was glad to see her again. B.C.'s date was a little on the heavy side, but had a pretty face. She was Cindy, and Debby said that this was Cindy's first year at the camp. She and B.C. were tentative about each other, but were trying to get acquainted.

They all went swimming again and sat on the dock for a while longer, and then the boys decided it was time to put in the motorboat. They would have to trail it to the head of the lake, where there was a launching ramp on the creek. The girls thought they would just as soon sun-bathe on the dock, so Matt and B.C. were off to launch the boat. The boat was impressive—white fiberglass, shining new, with blue and red stripes. The motor was impressive too. There would be no problem pulling two skiers except that the lake was pretty small.

They got the boat launched and parked the trailer. The motor started and let off a satisfactory roar. Matt took the wheel and they were off down the lake at full speed.

The girls were sun-bathing on their beach towels when Matt aimed straight at the dock, veered off at the last minute and sent a solid sheet of water over both of them. They sat up, undecided whether to be mad or not. Matt sped down the lake almost to the dam before turning around. He made another pass and sent another sheet of water over the dock. This time it was too much. "Debby, where did you get these damn cowboys? I'm not sure I want to go out in a boat with them. I'm not all that crazy about boats anyway. My beach towel is soaking wet, and I think my suntan lotion got washed off the dock."

"Oh, Matt's not too bad. I've known him before. He's really not much of a cowboy. I guess he was just showing off his new boat. I don't know about the muscle man; he's right good-looking, but he does seem to like his muscles. I wish he would quit sucking in his stomach and sticking out his chest. I don't think Matt knows him very well either. They've just been rooming together this last quarter."

"Well, if they make one more pass at this dock, I'm going to go up, get dressed, and demand to be taken back to the camp."

There were no more passes, however, and Matt pulled up quietly and tied the boat to the dock. The girls fussed a little but decided they weren't real mad, and prepared to go boat riding. The boys replenished their beers and B.C. got behind the wheel.

They made a couple of turns at high speed, having to slow down at the dam. About the third time, B.C. ran straight at the dam at full speed, expecting to make a close turn. He asked Matt, "What's past those arches anyway, Matt?"

"Well, B.C., there's just more lake. You can go through there if you want to."

Before Matt could explain that the arches were on top of a fifty-foot dam, B.C. headed the boat at top speed toward the center arch. There were about six inches of water going over the dam, and the boat cleared without even scraping. They had neglected to lock the motor down, so the lower unit kicked up, and they were over the dam and airborne. Three boys sitting in a pickup truck on top of the dam said that the boat shot out of the arch and seemed to hang momentarily in mid-air before settling down into the valley in pretty much the same position. They came down with an enormous splash into a small pool in the creek. For a moment there was absolute silence. B.C. was still holding a can of beer that was still half full; he took a deep gulp. Cindy turned toward him, "You absolutely have got to be the stupidest son of a bitch I have ever met. My back hurts. Get me out of here. Now!"

Matt found his voice. "Take it easy, Cindy. It was an accident. There's help coming."

The boys from the pickup truck were scrambling down the creek bank, and a few minutes later they were helping the girls out of the boat. Nobody seemed to be bleeding, and with the help of their rescuers the girls made it back to the road. Matt had a short conference with the driver. "They are from Camp Desoto; if they feel like going back now, I'd appreciate if it you'd take them. Maybe they ought to go to the hospital in Fort Payne."

Cindy muttered something and Debby said, "I think we're going to be all right if you'll take us back to the camp. We've got a nurse who can check us."

There were no goodbyes, and Matt and B.C. were left standing in the roadway.

"We might as well check the boat," Matt said. "I'm not sure what I'm going to tell my father."

They climbed back down to the creek. The boat was sitting in an upright position and didn't appear to have suffered serious damage. The lower unit of the motor was bent, but Matt figured it might be repaired. On the other hand, getting the boat out of the creek was going to be a problem he couldn't handle. Maybe the boat dealer could look after it. They climbed back up to the roadway, but no one was in sight. "B.C., if we go back by the road it's nearly four miles to the cabin. If we go the other way, past the old hotel, it's not so far, but we'll have to swim across the lake."

"My back hurts, but I think I can swim across the lake. I don't know about walking four miles."

Past the remains of the old hotel, they walked down through the bushes and swam across to the cabin. There was still beer in the ice box. They sat in the rockers on the porch and drank the beer.

"Matt, what do you think's going to happen?"

"Well, I'm not sure, but my father is probably going to sue you. Cindy may sue you, and Camp Desoto is going to banish us for life. Why don't you walk back and get the car and trailer? It's only about a mile. I'm ready to go back to school. I don't want to be here when my father comes. I'd rather call him on the phone."

B.C. had trouble getting out of bed Monday morning. His back was sore and his ego bruised. He never really thought he was smart, but this business of everybody calling him stupid was a little depressing. Now he was probably going to get sued by Matt's father and maybe by Cindy. She wasn't a bad-looking girl, especially in a bathing suit, but she had come down hard on him. He got dressed and didn't even look in the mirror. Matt had gotten out early, and they hadn't discussed their accident any farther.

Tuesday was more of Monday, and not much better. What happens when you get sued? Somebody had told him that the sheriff came and brought papers which had to be looked after. He would have to tell his mother and father and probably it would be in the newspaper. It was really all Matt's fault. They really ought to be suing Matt.

On Wednesday B.C. opened his post box and there it was. From Camp Desoto, "an outstanding camp for girls," Mentone, Alabama. The letter smelled pretty good, but B.C. was suspicious. Besides being barred for life, maybe the camp was going to sue him too. He carried it back to his room and set it on his chest of drawers. He didn't need any more bad news. He thought about it pretty hard, though; after all, a letter that smelled that good couldn't be all bad. He tore off the end of the envelope and pulled out the letter.

"Dearest B.C., I am feeling fine. My back wasn't hurt after all, and I taught the archery class this afternoon. I realize that it was all an accident and certainly not your fault. I would certainly like to see you again. Maybe you and Matt can come up for the weekend. Love, Cindy."

B.C. got up, squared his shoulders and looked in the mirror.

The P-G Special

HUGH AND PIGGY were hooking up the trailer when I drove up. The trailer looked big, even empty. Piggy had designed it especially for my twenty-five-foot keel boat, *Edinchip*, and when loaded, the boat towered over Piggy's small pickup truck. This morning we were going to the Harrison Bay Marina on Lake Chickamauga, north of Chattanooga, to haul *Edinchip* out and bring her down to the Atlanta Yacht Club on the Allatoona. She had been at Chickamauga for two years, and I was ready for a change of scenery; furthermore, the Allatoona is much nearer to my home in Rome.

Piggy's little truck looked old and frail. He saw me looking at it and put his hand on the hood where an ornament had once been. "This is a good truck," he said. "The odometer got turned over twice, and it quit a long time ago. No need to worry about this truck." We started toward Chattanooga.

I closed my eyes and tried to doze, but between the truck and trailer there was a good bit of noise. It was a summer day, and we had the windows down and, of course, no air conditioning. "Piggy," I said, "what kind of truck is this, anyway?" He gave this question serious consideration, but after a while he said, "Well, Dudley, that's hard to say. I traded an old Evinrude 25 for it, and that was a long time ago. The motor was running, but the truck wasn't, and it took us a while to get it going. We had to put on a lot of parts, some new and some used, and do a little welding. The fellow I got it from said it was a Chevrolet, but you

54

couldn't put much stock in anything he said. I never did see him again, so I guess the Evinrude ran all right. It did have a Chevrolet motor, but that's been gone awhile. I put in a G.M.C. that I got from a wreck, and it runs good. When anything happens, I keep putting in new parts, and it gets better and better.''

He smiled and said, "To answer your question, I guess you would have to say that this is a P-G Special Piggy Green Special."

The P-G Special pulled into the parking lot at Harrison Bay, and I went back to check the boat. *Edinchip* was sitting quietly in her slip, and I noticed that the varnish was peeling again. I swore to myself that this time I would paint the damn cabin and never buy another can of varnish. There was a nice breeze coming in from the lake, and I wondered why I was moving her. We took down the mast and lashed it across the cabin top. I knew I was going to get wet, so I changed into my swimming trunks and after a while succeeded in getting the motor started. Piggy backed the truck down the ramp, and when I motored up, he was waiting for me. The truck's back wheels were in the water, but the trailer cradles weren't even wet. Getting the boat out was going to be a job. Some of the bystanders were commenting on the impossibility of putting the boat up on the cradles, but we had done this before, and I wasn't too worried. I got out our chain and hooked it to the trailer while Piggy was taking the trailer loose from the truck. Most of the trailer disappeared quietly in the water, and all I had to do was get the boat in the right position. This wasn't all that easy, for the trailer showed some tendency to float. However, a couple of small boys who had been swimming came to our assistance, and before long we had *Edinchip* positioned over the cradles. I hollered for Piggy to tighten the chain, and everything seemed to be working fine. *Edinchip* settled down on the cradles in reasonably good position, and Piggy put the P-G Special in gear. The motor roared and the chain tightened, but nothing much else happened. Piggy got out and kicked the front tire and pulled off his cap. He tried it again, but this time a cloud of blue smoke came out of the hood, and we stopped operations. By this time a good many boats and trailers were lined up waiting to use the ramp. The fellow next in line, without saying anything, unhooked his trailer and hooked his truck to the front end of the P-G Special. I stood out of the way, and, with a mighty heave, the two trucks pulled *Edinchip* up on the lot. There was a small cheer from the assembled spectators as we cleared the ramp and pulled over to the side of the parking lot. The marina operator came over with my receipt for the slip rental and wished me good luck. *Edinchip* sat high in her cradles and towered over the P-G Special. "If you don't have far to go and it's all downhill, you may make it," he said and went back about his business. It was time to go, and we started.

I-75 south of Chattanooga is hilly, but there are no mountains, and we chugged along at a fairly good clip. The P-G strained mightily on the hills but kept going. Downhill, the 5,000 pounds of *Edinchip* gave us a mighty push, which was a little scary at times.

We weren't too far from the Red Top Mountain exit when the state patrol stopped us. The Special had a sign on the side which proudly stated that it belonged to the P-G Marine Supply Company. The young patrolman was friendly, and we all shook hands and started to talk about boats. He had heard of Piggy, but stopped smiling as he inspected our outfit. "Mr. Green," he said, "I know you are an experienced boatman, but do you realize that there are no brakes on this trailer and no stop lights and no turn signals?" Piggy looked pained and began a long, lame explanation based on the fact that we were ready to leave Rome, and he hadn't had time to do the necessary work. The young guy looked unhappy, but finally asked us where we were going. I joined the conversation and said, "Officer, we are only going to Red Top Mountain and will get the boat and trailer off the road and park it in the lot." He looked dubious but finally said, "I ought to run you in, but I'm going to escort you up to the

Red Top turnoff and hope that you don't kill yourself or some-body else before you get this rig parked. You do know that the road is pretty steep going down to the lake, and this outfit could get away from you." We agreed with everything he said and proceeded slowly under police escort to the Red Top exit.

The road from I-75 to Allatoona Lake goes down a steep hill with a number of fairly sharp curves. Subdued by the recent interview with the patrol officer, we started slowly, but when we started down the hill, *Edinchip* began to push pretty hard. In a few minutes we were going pretty fast and gaining speed. I looked at Piggy and he pushed on the brake pedal. After a little resistance, it went to the floor.

"No brakes," he said, "they're gone."

"For gosh sake, Piggy, put it in gear. We've got to get this thing slowed down."

He put the gear lever in second but nothing happened. "No gears either," he said. "Look out the window at the rear wheel."

I looked out. The wheel was obviously now disconnected from the truck and at the very end of the axle and wobbling. I don't think I hollered, but I probably raised my voice. "Piggy, the damn wheel is coming off!"

"I guess the cotter key broke off and the nut is gone," he said. "Hold on."

There were no handles or seat belts on the P-G Special, so I shut my eyes and waited for something to happen. Nothing happened except we seemed to go faster and faster, and Piggy was having a problem with the steering wheel.

"Look at the wheel," he said, and I looked. It was still at the end of the axle and still wobbling, but still on. We were almost on the bridge now, and we began to slow down. We coasted to a stop in the middle of the big steel bridge over Allatoona Creek. The wheel was still on, but barely. We got out and looked at the wheel, which was sitting at the very end of the axle at an ominous angle.

"We've got to have help," Piggy said. "I'll walk over to the marina and call Hugh. You stay here and direct traffic."

I stationed myself behind the trailer, took off my hat and began to wave it at oncoming traffic. Waving at traffic looks like a fun thing when somebody else is doing it, but it was very hot, and after a while I began to get tired. I finally decided to sit in the truck and rest for a few minutes. I got in and had just laid my head back on the seat and shut my eyes when there was a screech of brakes behind the trailer. I got out. There was a car at an angle behind the trailer, and *Edinchip*'s mast was extended some distance over the car. Fortunately, it was a small, low car, or it would have been impaled on the mast. The car's occupants and I exchanged a few unpleasantries, then they backed up and, under my direction, went around *Edinchip* and on their way. I decided that, having escaped from the P-G Special, I would take no more chances, and that the traffic would have to take care of itself. I walked on across the bridge and sat down under a tree and waited for Piggy to come back.

Maybe thirty or forty minutes later he reappeared, walking slowly with a bottled drink in either hand. "Hugh's not happy, but he's coming. He has a big toolbox on his truck and we ought to be all right. I thought you were directing traffic."

"I was, but it's hot and dangerous out there, and I nearly got run over once."

It took Hugh about an hour. The traffic took care of itself, but there were periodic screams of burning rubber and blowing horns. No officers of the law appeared, so we continued to sit under the tree. Hugh had a number of uncomplimentary things to say, including the observation that in the future we should stay at home and watch television. The repair to the P-G Special was very simple. Hugh jacked up the axle and pushed the wheel back in its place, screwed on a new nut, added a cotter key and we were ready to go.

The Atlanta Yacht Club was only a couple of miles down the road, and we parked *Edinchip* in the lot. We were both too tired to do anything more than put rocks under the trailer wheels and start back toward Rome. It was late in the afternoon, and we weren't far from Cartersville. I shut my eyes, leaned back in the seat and said, "Piggy, it's been a long day." He didn't answer immediately, and I felt the truck slow down.

"It's going to be longer," he said. We coasted to the side of the road and I noticed that there was a red light on the dash.

"No oil," he said. I knew it was my turn. I got slowly out of the truck and thought we must be at least two miles from Cartersville.

"It will take at least a gallon of thirty-weight," he said. I started slowly toward Cartersville. As I started walking he called after me, "Try to get back before dark. The truck doesn't have any lights."

The *Good Omen*

T HERE WAS A LADY sitting in the cockpit, apparently waiting for someone; certainly she was the owner, waiting to check us out. Both of us were already committed. I had accepted the boat based on pictures and information furnished, and she had approved my résumé and accepted my deposit. She looked like a pleasant lady—outdoorsy and well-tanned. She greeted us and asked us aboard. Paul and I identified ourselves, and she said she was Mrs. West and that this was the *Good Omen*.

The boat was a genuine Chesapeake bug-eye, forty years old and forty-two feet long, not counting an eight-foot bowsprit. The old ketch looked wonderful—a new coat of white paint gleaming, the wooden spars bright with new varnish. Paul said several nice things about how the boat looked, and Mrs. West seemed pleased.

"We have tried to keep her in good condition, and we think we have," Mrs. West said. "My husband and I spend a good bit of time aboard—most of it keeping things shipshape. We are planning to take her across the gulf stream sometime next month, probably out to Abaco and Hopetown."

I looked at the rig. I had never sailed a ketch, and it looked fairly complicated, but I thought we would make out. I was a little awed by the bowsprit and wondered how my crew would feel when they saw the cable hanging under the bowsprit on which they were supposed to stand when tending the jib. It would be a gutsy thing while under sail in a good breeze. They would need to wear life vests and be hooked up to the life lines. Even then, I thought, maybe we would not do it. Bowsprits are out of my line; I would just as soon the boat end at the bow. But everything looked in great shape, and a forty-two foot ketch with a bowsprit would be a challenge.

We talked a little about the boat, and I told Mrs. West that I had cruised several times on the Chesapeake and that this would be my third trip out of Dinner Key. We were in the marina at Dinner Key, just south of Miami, and I thought she looked a little relieved. I told her that we planned to go down in the Keys, maybe some outside and some inside, but that we had no planned itinerary. I have never had an itinerary I could keep up with on a sailboat trip; I planned to go south for three or four days and then turn around and come back to the dock. That seemed to satisfy her, but she made me promise not to try for the Bahamas. "If someone is going to cross the stream, we like to know about it in advance and be in on the planning," she said. "It can get pretty rough when the wind is from the northeast, and we try to take good care of the *Omen.*"

A big part of bare-boat chartering is the checkout. Mrs. West got out the equipment list and we checked every item. If anything were missing when we got back, it would be our responsibility. She then checked Paul and me out on the operation of the boat. We went over everything—halyards, fuel tanks, water tanks, batteries, head—the whole thing. Paul and I are both pretty good sailors for landlubbers, and when she finished I thought we could handle the *Omen* in reasonable weather.

"I have two more people coming," I said. "They are driving down from Rome and should be here sometime this afternoon. They are bringing a lot of equipment, including food, but we may end up spending tonight at the dock or we may run over to No Name Harbor and spend the night."

Mrs. West left, saying she would be back before dark, and Paul and I relaxed in the cockpit.

I hadn't expected Claborn and Dr. Ragsdale until late in the afternoon, but they showed up before we had had much of a nap. They were loaded with bags and boxes of equipment. They would do the housekeeping, while Paul and I handled the boat. Dr. Ragsdale's hobby is cooking, and he had elected himself chef and volunteered to bring some food and be responsible for buying the rest. As skipper, this certainly suited me; when cruising, I am generally a sandwich-and-canned-stew man. Paul and I started stowing the gear, and the doctor was off to the grocery store for additional supplies.

"Don't forget the liquor store," I told them. "Bourbon, scotch, or gin is all right with me, but remember we are going to be gone a week, and we don't know about supplies in the Keys." When I am skipper, I have a strict rule about no whiskey until the anchor is down or we are tied to a dock, but after that a reasonable amount of drinking is allowable.

As it was only about 4:00 in the afternoon, we decided to shove off and spend the night in No Name Harbor across Biscayne Bay from Dinner Key. No Name is a small protected anchorage on Key Biscayne, not far from the lighthouse. Aside from being small and generally crowded, it is a pleasant place to anchor. Paul is an excellent crew, and we had the *Omen* ready to go by the time Claborn and the doctor got back.

Claborn and the doctor returned with groceries and liquor, and we were ready to leave. Most boats of forty feet are steered by a wheel, but the *Omen* had an enormous curved tiller, brightly varnished and boasting some intricate marlinspike cording. This suited me fine; I am used to a tiller, but not one this size. We had the motor running when Mr. and Mrs. West arrived to see us off. I was a little nervous, but the traffic was light and I managed to back out of the slip and get headed out without any problem. The *Omen* was a little sluggish answering her helm, but Paul and I practiced a little bit on the way across the bay. Before we got to No Name we could see a forest of masts sticking up, so in lieu of a little more practice maneuvering, we decided to stay in the bay.

I ran up the shore of Key Biscayne and anchored just off the channel. It wasn't a great anchorage, but it would have to do.

I was below mixing a highball when suddenly there was a considerable commotion on deck. The coast guard had arrived on one side and a small, unmarked boat on the other. I thought these people would ask to come aboard, but the two men from the unmarked boat climbed aboard without any permission from me. They flashed some sort of credentials and wanted to know who we were and what we were doing there. I was a little irritated with these proceedings and announced that we were law-abiding American citizens and wanted to know why in hell we were being boarded. One of these fellows went below and started looking around, and the other one announced that they were treasury agents. He said, ''We want to know what you guys are doing anchored 200 yards off Key Biscayne and directly off President Nixon's vacation hideaway. The president happens to be in residence, and we don't want any strange boats anchored off the beach.'' He motioned toward a modest brick house which had a large American flag flying from the pole in the yard. ''We want you to move, or we will move you,'' he said.

Dr. Ragsdale said, ''Well, I guess we'd better go.''

We pulled up anchor and started the motor. We settled for a terrible anchorage between No Name and the lighthouse, but it was nearly dark, and we had little choice. I took a bearing on the lighthouse and on a channel marker and hoped for the best. We finally had a couple of drinks and some sandwiches. The doctor was disappointed at not being able to show off his culinary skills, but I assured him that the next night we would have candles and wine. I didn't know he had actually bought some. It was an uncomfortable night, and I was up several times checking the bearings. The anchor seemed to be holding, and that was that.

Daylight comes early on a sailboat, especially if you haven't slept much. The doctor said that due to the boat's motion, he didn't feel that he could handle bacon and eggs, so we had orange juice and corn flakes. It was a beautiful day.

"Today, my crew," I announced grandiloquently, "we will sail beyond the sunset and the baths of all the western stars."

Paul muttered, "It's too early for poetry, Skipper. Let's get the sails up."

We got them up and headed in the general direction of Bimini. The wind was just right. The stream seemed quiet, and I was tempted to break my promise to Mrs. West and head for the Bahamas. The old ketch behaved beautifully, even though she was a little sluggish in coming about. It was a good day to be sailing on the Atlantic. We headed for no place in particular, but practiced coming about and maneuvering, and everybody got a chance to take the helm and see how a forty-two-foot sailboat handles in the ocean.

We ate sandwiches while underway, and finally headed back, taking the channel through Stiltsville, that remarkable collection of shacks built on pilings seemingly in the middle of Biscayne Bay. Late that afternoon we cleared Featherbed Bank through the outer channel and anchored in eight feet of beautifully clear water off the north end of Elliott Key. It's a good anchorage and popular with local yachtsmen. We had plenty of company, but it was not too crowded.

The doctor outdid himself. We had fresh salad, beef stroganoff, and wine by candlelight. This doesn't happen very often on a sailboat.

There is a small state park and marina on the west side of Elliott Key, and we decided to stop for more ice. It was not far from our anchorage, so we didn't put up the sails, but motored along the shoreline to the park. The park had a small harbor with docks and slips and looked like a good place to stop. I headed the *Omen* into a vacant slip, cut the motor, and thought I was making a good landing when we came to a sudden halt. The slip had not been designed for the *Omen's* nine-foot beam and we were stuck solidly in the slip. Since it was obvious that we weren't going anywhere very soon, I suggested that they go ahead and get the ice and whatever else we needed.

I put the motor in reverse, but nothing happened. Paul got out and pushed with the motor in reverse and still nothing. We decided to wait for reinforcements. Claborn and the doctor eventually came back loaded with ice and cookies, and with the help of a couple of bystanders and the motor in reverse, the *Good Omen* came loose from the grip of the slip, and we proceeded down the bay under full sail.

The next two days were great. One night we anchored off Pumpkin Key, and the next day went through the cut near the Ocean Reef Club and out into the Atlantic. We anchored off Pennekamp Reef and tried to skin dive, but the water was too rough. After a little ocean sailing we headed back into the bay. Below Tavernier the channel becomes very narrow, and we ended up motoring to the marina on Plantation Key. It was a nice place—good docks, a motel, and a restaurant with good seafood. We decided we had gone south far enough, so after a couple of nights we headed north again.

Somebody demanded that we try to catch some fish, so late in the afternoon we anchored in Card Sound and put out the fishing lines. I am not much of a fisherman and tend to be very pessimistic; however, we began to catch fish at an alarming rate. I think they were croakers, but maybe there were some others mixed in. Anyway, they were declared to be edible, and the doctor fried fish for the next couple of meals.

There is a drawbridge across Jew Fish Creek where the road from Homestead crosses to the Keys. It was a nice day with a light breeze out of the north. We pulled over to the marina just south of the bridge for a rest stop and a sandwich. Back on board, I blew the horn and the bridge opened promptly. We motored through the bridge without incident, but about a hundred yards north of the bridge, the motor quit. We began to drift back toward the bridge, which was now closed and full of traffic. There was no time to check the motor, and I hollered for Paul to put the anchor overboard. It was a good big anchor and quickly held, but by that time the bridge tender and I were

looking each other in the eye. He shrugged his shoulders and pointed to the traffic and seemed to be wishing us luck. The anchor had snagged on something, and we were in no immediate danger of taking out the *Good Omen*'s mast on the bridge. Paul bent over the motor, did something, and it immediately started. He looked at me and said, ''Somebody cut off the gas line.''

It's good practice to cut off the gas line for an overnight stop, but I had not expected anyone to cut off the gas line for a rest stop and sandwich. It was my responsibility, all right, because I was the skipper, but I never found out who had cut the line off, and nobody volunteered. We now had the motor running and were in good shape except that the big, expensive anchor was snagged solidly on something. It became obvious that it was not coming up and we had no scuba gear—nor experienced divers for that matter. I finally gave the order to cut the line, waved at the bridge tender, trying to convey the idea that we would come back and get it. We were on our way again, but we had come close to doing serious damage to the boat and possibly ourselves.

This time No Name Harbor was not so crowded, and we spent

our last night aboard enjoying a light breeze and the doctor's finest cooking. He had saved some wine, and the candles came out again.

The next morning we headed back across the bay to Dinner Key and the *Omen*'s slip. The boat was in excellent shape, but I hated to tell Mrs. West about the missing anchor. I hated it even worse when she told me it would cost $150 to replace. About a month later, she got the anchor back from the bridge tender who had salvaged it, so, after paying him a reward, we got most of our money back.

Voyage of the *Fat Girl*

TRAFFIC WAS HEAVY at the Miami airport as we let Dianne and Dodie out at the gate. They would spend a week with Dodie's parents in the Dominican Republic. If all went well, we would then pick them up at the airport. They gave us the date and flight number, and we wished each other well. Evelyn and I headed for the Coral Reef Yacht Club, where we were to meet the yacht broker and owner of the *Fat Girl*. I had a week's bare boat charter and was anxious to get going. It was getting a little late, so we decided to do a little shopping and spend the night at the dock; we would start early the next day.

The owner and the broker of the yacht were on board when we arrived. The *Fat Girl* was a fat twenty-eight-foot sloop, but she looked clean and comfortable. We introduced each other around and admired the boat. Once you rent a boat, you might as well admire it, because you have to sign a contract and pay the charter fee in advance. The owner was a youngish athletic type with a deep suntan. He told us he was spending most of his time in the Bahamas living aboard, but that he had come back hoping to pick up a few charters. Generally, the owners just take you "as is" once the contracts have been signed, but this fellow wanted to check me out. He started the motor, and I took the wheel. The *Fat Girl* had a beautiful mahogany wheel with real spokes like you see in pictures—not the stainless steel kind mostly in use nowadays. He wanted me to take over, so I eased out of the slip, hoping that the *Fat Girl* had a responsive helm. She did, and we headed out into the bay.

The owner was serious, and I got the idea that he hadn't chartered his boat very much.

"Why don't you give me the wheel, and you put up the sails," he said. This was no big deal. I told him to head into the wind and then winched up the main and then the jib. Some people like to do the jib first, but I feel better with the main. The wind was light, but we came about a couple of times and the owner seemed satisfied. As we headed back toward the dock, he even furled the sails and handled the lines. It was Saturday, and I told him I expected to be back at the club by the following Saturday. I had a telephone number to call in case of an emergency. We were ready. Or at least almost ready.

It was late afternoon and I wasn't feeling too well, but I was not about to admit it. The Coral Reef Yacht Club is a nice club— they let us go in to dinner. Things were fairly formal, and jackets were required. The waiter pointed me to a closet full of odd jackets, and I found one which was a fair fit, and we went in.

I didn't have a very good night and was afraid I was coming down with something. This trip had been planned a long time, and I put the thought of getting sick out of my mind, or at least tried to. I didn't tell Evelyn I wasn't feeling well, and the next morning we shoved off and headed down the bay. There wasn't much wind, but since we had chartered a sailboat, we put up the sails and headed in the general direction of Key West. It was a slow go, and it was mid-afternoon before we cleared Featherbed Bank by the outer channel.

The north end of Elliott Key is a popular anchorage, but we found a spot and dropped anchor. Normally I would swim to the beach, but by now I was feeling worse than before. It was a bad night, and I finally confessed that I was running a fever and thought we should go back. It's not far from Elliott to Coral Reef, and under full power we were back in less than three hours. The manager was sympathetic. "Dr. Richardson, one of our members, is down by the pool. I'll be glad to ask him if he would mind seeing you."

I didn't mind at all; I wanted to see somebody. In a few minutes the doctor, still in his swimming trunks, came up and had a quick look at me.

"This is real unofficial," he said, "but you've got a bug that needs attending to. Go on over to the University Hospital Emergency Room, and tell them you are one of my patients and that I said to look after you real well. Most of those people know me, and I think you'll get good care."

"Doctor, I appreciate you looking at me. Will you send me a bill?"

"I think you're going to feel better pretty quickly, so let's not worry about it. If you get worse, I'll probably see you anyway. Maybe you'll perk up and get back on the boat this week."

The people at the emergency room were friendly and helpful. I told them I was Dr. Richardson's patient, and that seemed to help.

"It's just a bug. Maybe a couple of days and you'll be back on the boat," said the nurse. She gave me a shot and some pills. "The pharmacy isn't open, so these pills are on the house. My services aren't though, and you can pay on the way out. Go lie down somewhere for a couple of days and take your pills, and if you don't get better, come on back and we'll put you in."

When you're a long way from home, a few kind words help. I paid my bill, and we found a small neighborhood motel. The *Fat Girl* was sitting in her slip growing barnacles, and I was frustrated. I spent two nights in that damned motel waiting to get well, and on the second morning I declared myself recovered and told Evelyn we were going back out. She wasn't happy about it, but I don't think she wanted to spend another day cooped up with me in the motel, either.

The boat was ready, and we took off heading south. There wasn't much wind, and I had had enough of the bay north of Featherbed. The *Fat Girl* could do nearly seven knots under power, and I opened the throttle to full speed. Fortunately, the bay was pretty quiet, and we didn't get bounced a lot. Mac had told me about the Ocean Reef Club and said we ought to stop there. To get to the club you go outside into Hawk Channel and down the coast a couple of miles. The channel into the club is well marked, and there was no problem. The dock master drove up in a golf cart and presented us with dinner menus. It all looked pretty fancy, including the price, but the dock master turned out to be from Resaca, Georgia, and we had some mutual acquaintances. He told me I needed to register, and off we went to the club in his golf cart. They had hotel rooms, but after two nights in a motel I elected to stay at the dock. This was a terrible decision as it turned out, but we did have a good dinner. Summertime is slow season at Ocean Reef, and I didn't have to wear a jacket, although I suspect they had a closetful hidden somewhere. The dock master told me there might be a few mosquitoes and wished us luck. He could have gone into a little more detail because about dark they began to arrive—not singly or in pairs, but in swarms. I have never seen so many mosquitoes in one place: big mosquitoes and probably little mosquitoes. We had come prepared, I thought. We smeared each other with 6-12 ointment, but this seemed to whet their appetites, and if any were discouraged, there were plenty of others to take their places. I put my clothes back on, including long pants and a long-sleeved shirt. The *Fat Girl* had come equipped with sheets and pillow cases, and after a while I put a pillow case over my head and considered my alternatives. They were pretty limited. I could lie there and suffer, or suffocate to death under the pillow case. I decided that enough was enough and walked up to the club house to rent a room. It was closed and the door locked. Everyone had turned in for the night. Back at the dock, I considered the hazards of nighttime navigation and decided against it. I crawled back under the covers, determined to stay there. I did stay there for a while until Evelyn punched me and said, "There's something trying to come aboard." She had been sitting in the cockpit, apparently having given up on getting any sleep. I got the flashlight, and sure enough, climbing up our dock line was a big blue crab. I don't think he really wanted to make it to the cockpit, and I doubt if he could have, but he sure looked ugly and seemed to be trying hard to get aboard.

"I am definitely going home, and I will never get on another sailboat as long as I live," Evelyn said.

I took the boathook and knocked the crab back into the water, but there was no assurance that he or other members of his family intended to stay there. I gave Evelyn the flashlight and the boathook and went back to bed.

Daylight finally came. I scribbled a note to the club manager giving my name and address and suggesting that the bill for dinner and dockage be forwarded to me. The club was still closed tight, and I stuck it under the door.

We were back in the bay as soon as we could get there. There was a nice breeze, and I wanted to put as much distance between us and the mosquitoes as possible. We anchored in the middle of the bay and went to sleep. There were no mosquitoes, and we slept soundly. It must have been two or three o'clock in the afternoon when Evelyn woke me. "You ready for a sandwich?"

I was, and we had lunch. We were both rested, and I felt better. "Somewhere, somewhere tonight, we will go to a motel. I am not sure where, but I will find one."

"You sure as hell better," she said. "I've had it with the *Fat Girl.*" We put cushions on the floor of the cockpit, smeared suntan lotion on each other, and made love. If any boats came by, I didn't notice. Maybe the trip would work out.

Tavenier seemed to be the best possibility. I figured there would be a motel of some sort. I started the motor and headed south. We hadn't done much sailing, but maybe we could sail on the way back to Miami.

There didn't seem to be much going on in what I assumed was Tavenier Harbor. There were a few houses and one or two buildings—one that looked like a marina. I didn't see any channel markers, so I headed straight in. Two or three hundred yards from the marina dock there was a stick poking out of the water with a milk jug on top of it. I mentally tossed a coin and decided left. I thought I heard the *Fat Girl* sigh as we slowly went into the mud bank. Not sand or rock, just soft, gooey, gray mud. I tried to reverse, but it was too late. We had settled in. We tried a few other things, including cussing, none of which worked.

Evelyn looked pretty sad. "Try not to worry about this," I said. "We're absolutely not in any danger. The boat is fine, we have plenty to eat and drink aboard and could spend the night if we had to. We are practically to the marina, and somebody is bound to come along and help us. I solemnly promise that we will spend the night at the motel, and tomorrow we'll start home. Try to relax—we'll just have to wait to be rescued."

I lay down, pulled my cap over my eyes, and tried to take a nap. I think I actually dozed a little before a voice said, "Hello there! You folks got a problem?" There was a rowboat alongside manned by a nice-looking woman with long blonde hair, accompanied by a small girl with long blonde hair. The lady said, "I live over there," motioning to a house on the beach, "and saw you go aground. Thought I might be of some help."

"We definitely could stand some help. I guess I misread the milk bottle."

"It's a shame we haven't marked the channel better. We have had some marks, but they have to be maintained, and the local people don't need any channel markers. I can't pull you off the bank myself, but I will row around to the marina and see if I can get Mr. Adams. He owns the marina and the motel, and if I can find him, I'm sure he'll come out and pull you off. He's going to charge you something, though, so be prepared." I thanked her, and she rowed away toward the marina.

Mr. Adams must have been at home, because it wasn't long until a big motorboat came out of the marina and headed our way. There wasn't a lot of conversation. Mr. Adams said, "Throw me your bow line." Fortunately, I had a bow line, which I threw and he caught. I thought he would pull us out the way we went in, but he tied our bow line to a cleat on the stern of the motorboat and yanked us sideways. We came off in a cloud of mud and were towed over to the marina dock.

"That'll be twenty-five dollars," he said.

I said, "Okay." We needed help. "We would like to spend the night at the motel if you have a room open."

"Practically all the rooms are open," he said. "This is not our busy season. The rooms are clean and air conditioned, but it's not a fancy place. If you want to go up to your room, I'll tie up the boat. I know number 3 is made up. We don't have any keys, so make yourself at home."

The motel was just behind the marina—basic concrete block, but the room was clean and the air conditioner worked. I was preparing to take another nap when Mr. Adams knocked on the door.

"Mrs. Dorsey—that's the lady in the rowboat—says for you folks to come to dinner at 7:00. They live in the second house down from the marina. Says they'll be expecting you." Mr. Adams apparently didn't expect a reply, and was already gone. We were both tired, but this was not a refusable invitation. We did have time to clean up a little.

The Dorseys' fairly modest home featured a large screened porch which practically hung over the water. It was easy to see how Mrs. Dorsey could spend a lot of time boat-watching, and I suspected that we were not the first people she had rescued. Mr. Dorsey greeted us at the door and led us into a big Florida room that joined the porch. He was in a wheelchair, and I got the impression he had been in it for a very long time. Mrs. Dorsey came in and asked us about drinks. She hadn't done anything to her hair, but I sort of like long, loose blonde hair, and she looked very nice.

We sat on the porch and chatted. We were all relaxed, and pretty soon we were on a first-name basis. John was a lawyer practicing in Tavenier. He explained that Tavenier was not the county seat, but that he had a good bit of business drawing wills and deeds and was specializing in handling real estate transactions. "It's not much," he said, "but our expenses are modest and I keep fairly busy. I had polio when I was a child, and it left me like this, but I get around pretty well and even do some sailing." He pointed to a small sailboat pulled up on the beach. "I can lift myself in and out, and I rigged up some lines and can generally get the boat in the water. It's a nice area, and I sail as often as I can."

Dinner was hamburgers and salad, which suited us fine. Afterward we went back on the porch and sat for a while. We had a nice visit, but it was soon time to leave; we promised to keep in touch. I think we did exchange Christmas cards once or twice, which is sort of the way those things go.

Evelyn was up early. Mr. Adams had no restaurant, so we went aboard and had our own orange juice and corn flakes. It was going to be a long day back to Coral Reef. I looked at the chart. It was nearly fifty miles, which is quite a way for a sailboat. It was early and there was no wind, which was just as well, since I figured we were going to have to motor most of the way anyway. This time I went on the proper side of the milk bottle, and we took off at full throttle. I didn't see anything of the

Dorseys, but we blew our horn and waved anyway. The *Fat Girl* was arranged so that I could put a deck chair behind the wheel, and I settled myself in for a lot of motorboating. Evelyn would take the wheel when I had to get up to stretch my legs or go to the head. We made good progress for several hours—up past Lock Harbor, through the drawbridge at Jew Fish Creek, through Barne's Sound, and past the cut that goes out to Ocean Reef Club. We needed to pick up Dianne and Dodie the next morning, but I didn't think that would be a problem. Evelyn was definitely not going to spend another night on *Fat Girl*, but we could go back to our motel.

Somewhere around Old Rhodes Key the motor started making strange sounds. I thought maybe we had been putting too much strain on it, so I cut our speed down a little, and it quieted down —at least for a while. Then it stopped completely. I punched the starter a few times. It would try to start and then give up. The motor of the *Fat Girl* was located under the cockpit floor, and I dutifully lifted the hatch and examined it by flashlight. It was big and looked like a very fine motor. Right then, it was giving off an odor of gas and oil and was smoking. I did know how to check the gas and oil, and they were both okay. I couldn't kick it because it was down in the bilge, so I closed the hatch, and Evelyn helped me put up the sails. Now there was a brisk ocean breeze, just where we wanted it, on the starboard beam. Soon we were at almost-full speed and heeling. This was really a lot better than motoring and almost as fast. After all, we had come to sail but had done nothing much but motor, and the trip was almost over. I worried a little about what I was going to do when I got to the dock, but we still had about twenty miles to sail, including going through Featherbed Bank Channel. Featherbed is an enormous sand bar that runs across the entire width of Biscayne Bay. In some places, the water is less than a foot deep at low tide. There are two channels—one out near Elliott Key, and the main channel in the middle of the bay. The main channel is well marked, but it would be sort of stupid to try to sail through if you had a motor. We didn't have a motor anymore, but we had a nice breeze, so in we went and through without any trouble.

A little over three hours later I sighted the markers into Coral Reef. The channel starts far out in the bay and looks like a picket fence. We turned into the channel; the wind was now directly behind us and still brisk. Getting to Coral Reef was not going to be a problem, but getting the boat into the slip was going to be a big problem. We sailed up to the club docks to have a look. The *Fat Girl*'s slip was empty, but there was no way I could sail her in. I jibed around a couple of times, trying to figure out what to do. We could probably anchor, blow the horn, and wave our arms, and wait to be rescued again. I didn't really want to be rescued again if I could avoid it. There is a sea wall across the cove from the yacht club, and I noticed a couple of people walking in the little park that borders the wall. I took a quick look at the chart and didn't see any reason I couldn't sail right up to the wall and get out. We went over pretty close and waved and hollered, but most of the people just went on about their business. One young guy finally waved and after some exchanges in sign language, he seemed to understand that I wanted him to take a line. I luffed the *Fat Girl* up to the wall and threw the line. Generally this maneuver doesn't go off too well without practice, but I threw the line fairly well, and he caught it and pulled us over. We dropped the sails and I went ashore.

I told him I needed to use the telephone, and he agreed to watch Evelyn and the boat until I got back. I tied the bow line to a palm tree and left. My luck was improving. The broker was in his office, and said he would be down right away. He did better than I expected, and in about fifteen minutes arrived by boat and towed us over to the club. In another fifteen or twenty minutes, we had the *Fat Girl* back in her slip and the lines secured.

We talked a little while we were getting our things together. He checked the boat and I told him that with the exception of a little mud we had picked up in Tavenier and the fact that the motor wouldn't run, the boat was fine. He checked around and said that as far as he was concerned he was ready to sign me off but that he had called the owner. The owner arrived and bounced aboard, looking very knowledgeable and not too friendly. He opened the hatch, crawled down and examined the motor with a flashlight, jiggled a few things, came back up and jiggled a few more things and confidently punched the starter. I smiled happily. The damn thing wouldn't start for him either.

Get the Anchor Down

CAPTAIN ANDERSON'S famous seafood restaurant appeared deserted. We were looking forward to some seafood, so I drove into the parking lot and looked at the door. The sign said "Open until 10:00." It is unusual for the Captain not to have a lot of customers, but it was a dreary November day with a light drizzle. Pat and I drove across the bridge to the marina where *Regardless* was docked. The cabin looked fairly neat, but everything was damp, and there was some mildew on the bulkhead.

It looked pretty dreary. I plugged in the little electric heater, and Pat handed over our luggage.

"We could stay in a motel, but I don't think it will be too bad once the heater gets going," Pat said.

We stowed our gear and walked across the street to the liquor store. It had started to rain, and I drove the car across the bridge to Captain Anderson's. The first floor door was open, but there didn't seem to be anybody around. We were looking for a waitress when the bottom of the liquor sack gave away. It made a loud pop, and there was glass and liquor all over the floor. A waitress now appeared and looked at the scene. "God," she said, "what a mess! It does smell like a pretty good brand. What is it? Bourbon?"

"It's just cheap whiskey," I said. "We drink a lot and can't afford expensive brands." Pat was just standing there holding the wet paper sack by the neck. He started to say something, but decided against it.

"Pat, I will pay for half of the old bottle, and half of the new bottle that you are about to go after. Why don't you go on back while I help this beautiful young woman clean up this mess." She was neither beautiful nor young, but she didn't look too bad. She was wearing a tag that said "Linda." She seemed to appreciate my remark, and said, "You fellows don't worry, I'll clean it up. Go sit down." Pat left, and I sat down near the scene of the disaster.

"What you fellows doing out on a night like this? We don't have a single customer, and even the Captain has gone home."

"Believe it or not, sweetie, we are yachtsmen and are staying on a sailboat just across the lagoon. If the weather stays like this, tomorrow we will go to a motel and watch television. If it gets better, we are going to sail out into the Gulf and maybe go to Destin or St. Joe."

"You guys fish, or what?"

"Honey, yachtsmen don't fish. We just sail around when the weather's good, and when it's bad we sit in the marina and complain."

"Sounds sort of silly to me," she said. "I thought everybody fished."

She had about cleaned up the floor, and I decided that she was better-looking than I thought. "Why don't you sit down and have a drink with us?"

"Lord, the Captain would fire me in a minute, and I need the job. I did like what you said, though. Exactly what was it?"

"I said that I would stay and help this beautiful young woman clean up this mess."

"Gee, I like that. My husband hasn't said anything nice to me in a long time." She looked around and sat on the edge of a chair.

"What time are you going to get off tonight? Maybe we could go yachting."

"No yachting tonight, honey. My husband's picking me up at 10:00, and I've got to serve you guys and get out of here. Maybe tomorrow night or some other night when he has to work late. I'd like to get rid of him anyway. He drinks and gambles all the time.''

Pat returned with a fresh bottle, which he held securely at the bottom. We fixed drinks and ordered the seafood platters. Linda came back and talked some more, but wouldn't sit down. Pat and I stuffed ourselves with fried seafood and hushpuppies washed down with bourbon and water. It was near 10:00 when we left, and I looked to see whether Linda's husband had arrived. We gave her a good tip—after all, she cleaned up our broken bottle.

It was raining pretty hard when we went out to the car. I had started the motor and started out when Linda came out of the door and waved at us. ''I lost my ride. My old man has to work an extra shift. I wonder if you guys would mind taking me home.'' Linda got in and I drove across the bridge and stopped at the marina. ''Pat, you might check out the boat. I'll take Linda home and be back in a little bit. I think she wants to learn a little more than yachting.''

I thought Pat might give me a problem, but he was full of fish and whiskey, and he got out and walked on toward the boat. He had what was left of the bottle, and I hoped he wouldn't use it all before I got back. I looked at Linda. The third drink had done it. She looked absolutely gorgeous. ''It is time to learn about yachting,'' I said. ''You'll have to study a little first before I can take you out on the boat.''

''You're silly,'' she said. ''It's late and I am tired, and besides, where could I learn anything about yachting tonight?''

''Well, it's a pretty complicated sport, but we would start maybe at the Holiday Inn.''

''You are silly. I don't hardly know you at all.''

''Well, I'm a real nice guy, and it's a rainy night, and your husband has to work an extra shift. We could at least visit and talk a little. Can I come on in?''

''Well, I guess that would be okay. Joe's not going to be home for a while.''

It was a little later.

"I know your name's Linda, but what goes with it?"

"Well, I've been married a couple of times before, but right now it is Zeigler. Linda is fine, but I don't know if I like Zeigler very well. He's mean as hell and drinks a lot. I don't know if things are going to work out too good. Honey, you haven't told me your name."

"I was afraid you were going to ask that. It's a problem I've had to live with. Luther Rosser Shackleford II."

"You're kidding," Linda said. "Nobody's got a name like that, but I guess nobody would make up a name like that either. How come they named you that?"

"Honey," I said, "money is a bad thing if you don't have it and sometimes a bad thing if you do. I was named after my mother's brother. He was an old bachelor and my mother thought he would leave me his money."

"It must have been an awful lot to name somebody that."

"As a matter of fact, when he was about eighty years old he married his nurse, and they lived happily for about three months before he died and left everything to her."

"You didn't get anything?"

"Well, you could say that, I guess, although his lovely young widow brought me over a few things she said Uncle Luther wanted me to have. Two meerschaum pipes, an Atwater-Kent radio, and a portrait of Martin Van Buren."

Linda looked puzzled. "I know what a pipe is, and my grandfather had an Atwater-Kent radio, but you lost me on that Van Buren. Who was he?"

"I'm not much up on him myself, but he was a president of the United States. I don't remember what number and I don't remember anything he did—either good or bad. My mother said Uncle Luther thought that he looked like the former president and was fond of telling people it was his great grandfather. Anyway, I'm named Luther Rosser Shackleford II, and I have a portrait of the late Martin Van Buren. I put it in a yard sale, but it didn't sell. He is a distinguished-looking old fellow—maybe I will tell people that he is my great-great-grandfather.

"Luther, are you about the silliest man I've ever met."

"Why don't you call me Rosser? I like that better and you are one of the best-looking young women I've run into in a long time."

"I do like you, Rosser. You talk so pretty. I'm glad I let you come in, but you absolutely have got to get out of here before 2:00."

&

Pat was in my bunk sound asleep and snoring loudly. I didn't see anything of the bottle, but it was late and there would be things to do tomorrow. I thought of waking him up but then decided against it and crawled into the V-bunk forward.

Pat woke me up pretty early. He was fooling around with the alcohol stove, but that stove is a delicate instrument, and I didn't think he was going to be able to light it. I was sleepy but awake. "Pat, leave the stove alone. I'll walk over to the Captain's and get a pot of coffee and donuts." Pat didn't look too good. "Go get the coffee," he said. "I need it—I'm not sure I can handle the donuts yet."

I walked across the bridge. The Captain's operation was in full swing. Lots of fishermen were having an early breakfast. I got a pot of coffee and some donuts and went over to the cash register. I said brightly to the attractive lady, "I wonder if you can tell me when Linda comes on?" She looked puzzled. "We don't have anybody by that name."

"But she waited on us last night and was wearing a silver nameplate that said 'Linda.' "

"Oh, that," she said. "Captain Anderson bought a bunch of nameplates a while back, and we sort of pass them around. Customers like to see them, and it really don't make much difference. We aren't supposed to socialize with the customers anyway."

I got the coffee and donuts and walked back across the bridge. *Regardless* looked good sitting in her slip. The rain had stopped, and it would be time to go very soon. I thought about Linda. "Damn," I said to myself. "That woman lied to me. I'm glad I didn't tell her my real name."

Pat declined a donut, and we sat in the cockpit drinking coffee. The sun was trying to come out. It was going to be a nice day. I looked at my watch. "Pat, it is time for me to go to the airport and pick up Luther Rosser Shackleford II. His plane should be landing almost any time."

"God, is that really his name?"

"Well, it's close," I said. "You clean up the cabin, and we'll be ready to go when I get back."

The plane was almost on time, and before long we were sailing down Grand Lagoon with a nice breeze on the quarter.

We had a brief discussion of our itinerary. The wind was blowing pretty hard, and we decided to stay inside and run down to the eastern tip of Shell Island. The island is mostly park and mostly uninhabited; access is by boat. The last mile or so at the eastern end is sand dunes and beach. Once upon a time somebody built a dock near the end of the island, and part of it was still there—enough for us to tie up to. Not a bad place to spend the night, except that off the end of the island is nothing much except the Gulf of Mexico, and if the wind came from the east, it was going to be uncomfortable.

Pat and Rosser walked over to the beach to look for shells. I am not much of a shell man, so I told them to go ahead. There are shells on Shell Island—they seem to wash up all along the outer islands of the Gulf Coast. The best specimens are in the gift shops, but people seem to have a lot of fun looking, and the walking is good exercise. I puttered around the boat, as most skippers do, and among other things I checked the alcohol stove. Alcohol stoves are used on boats because an alcohol flame can be put out with water and a gasoline fire can't. In general, alcohol stoves are reliable. Most have a pump that is used to generate pressure, and I noticed that the pump on mine didn't seem to be working very well. Inspection indicated that it wasn't working at all. The pad probably dried out. I'm not much of a mechanic, but I took it apart and applied a little oil—still nothing. My guests were going to be awfully disappointed with cold stew. I had three cans, but I suspected that one would be enough.

Rosser and Pat returned from the beach with a small paper sack full of shells. Most of them were broken, but they seemed happy and satisfied. I put them in the bilge where other shells have resided until I threw them out.

"What's for dinner, Skipper?" they both said at more or less the same time.

"Well, I was planning on rice and gravy and hot beef stew, but I'm having some trouble with the stove. It won't work. I suggest that you have a couple of drinks, and then things may not seem so bad." I heard some mumbling, but we had the drinks, and things didn't seem too bad until I opened the first can of stew. Anyone who has only seen stew hot and savory in a bowl has a rude surprise coming when they open a can and dump it out in a plate cold. The grease is congealed, generally on the top or bottom, and it looks pretty bad. It also tastes terrible. I have not eaten any dog food, but I imagine that the taste is similar. I mixed it around and made it look a little better, then divided it into three portions on paper plates. I gave everyone a piece of plain bread and a plastic fork.

"Does anyone feel the urge to give thanks for this food?" I said brightly. Pat and Rosser are both practicing Episcopalians. I think Pat mumbled something, and we bowed our heads. I managed to eat a couple of bites, washed down by my third highball. I don't think Pat managed any, but Rosser is a longtime Boy Scout master, hiker, and camper. I watched him clean his plate. "Rosser," I said, "we've got another can if you want me to open it."

"No, this is just fine," he said, "and I happen to have brought a moon pie for dessert. Sorry I didn't bring three.'' He reached in his jacket pocket and produced a moon pie, which he offered to divide. I declined, and I know Pat didn't eat any.

We sat on deck for a while until it was time to turn in. "Rosser, I am sorry to tell you, but you have the quarter berth. Pat is already in the V-berth and I am in the captain's berth. I think you will make out all right if you are not restless.'' A quarter berth is a contrivance in which the occupant's head and sometimes shoulders stick out into the cabin, and the rest of him or her extends back under the quarter deck. Fortunately, Rosser is a small man. It is generally conceded that the occupant of a quarter berth must determine in advance whether he is going to sleep on his back or his stomach, because once in the berth, rotation is generally impossible. There is certainly no tossing and turning. The quarter berth on *Regardless* is not too bad, and I figured Rosser just might be able to turn over if he wanted to bad enough.

Pat, who was already in the V-bunk, suddenly thought about the morning. "What do we do about coffee?'' he said. "I can eat cold stew if I have to, but I've got to have hot coffee in the morning. You're the skipper—what are you going to do about it?'' I turned my head and pretended I was asleep.

I smelled coffee—hot coffee—and it smelled good. I wondered where it came from. Rosser and Pat were sitting in the cockpit drinking it and looking happier than they had looked last night. They saw me sticking my head out of the hatch, and Pat remarked casually, "Do you think we ought to let him have any? Any captain that would serve his guests cold stew does not deserve a lot of consideration.'' Rosser stirred his coffee and said, "I guess we'd better fix him a cup. He's the only one who knows how to get back to the marina.''

I couldn't figure out how they heated the coffee until I saw it: there on the cockpit floor was last night's stew can; it was now half full of sand that Rosser had soaked with alcohol. It made a nice little stove and was admitting a cheerful blue flame. Rosser looked up, "You can't help but learn a few things after twenty years as a Scoutmaster." I wondered why he didn't heat the stew last night, but I guess he forgot to remember his scout training.

The coffee was good and hot, and we had some bread and jelly. "Rosser, this is an ingenious device; maybe we could get you a patent."

"Afraid not," Rosser said. "Actually, it's described in a Scoutmaster's handbook of camping. Never used it before, but it seems to work all right—at least on coffee, although I wouldn't want to try bacon and eggs on it."

We started the outboard and motored across to the Tyndall Yacht Club. This is a serviceman's club attached to the Tyndall Air Base on the mainland across the sound from where we had spent the night. We hoped for bacon and eggs, but we only got more coffee and some donuts. They also sold us some sandwiches, which we carried aboard for lunch.

It was time for a real sail—the wind was out of the west at maybe fifteen to twenty knots. The Gulf looked pretty rough, and we headed toward West Bay on nice close reach. We were taking a little spray, but the sun had come out and it was a great day for sailing. I put on my foul-weather gear, since the man at the tiller was going to get wet. We weren't having to tack, just a good close reach with the rail pretty far down—not everybody's thing, but it was what I had come to Florida for. After a while, I gave the tiller to Pat and went below to dry off a little. Rosser sat with his back to the bulkhead, pretty much out of the wind and spray. We were making good time but had nowhere in particular to go.

By 2:00 we were crossing the shipping lane and the main part of St. Andrews Bay. I figured we would go on up West Bay, maybe all the way to the intercoastal waterway, and find someplace to anchor for the night. Rosser took the helm, and Pat came below to dry off. *Regardless* was heeling about 20 percent and bouncing a lot. We were probably better off without bacon and eggs. I've never been really seasick, but I've had some guests who have had problems. I remember one who actually turned green and suffered to the point where we turned around and went back. Pat and Rosser seemed to be fine.

Pat touched me on the knee and said, "Your Honor, I have been yachting for two days and have spent two nights in that V-bunk which slopes at a peculiar angle. I am not complaining, but it would be nice to spend our last night in a motel. There must be one somewhere reasonably available."

"As a matter of fact, the Holiday Lodge is located in West Bay and has its own docks for visiting yachtsmen." I had been thinking about it myself and hoping somebody would ask. "I wouldn't mind a bed and hot shower myself. We'll look in at the Holiday Lodge when we get to West Bay." We held on for a while. I was enjoying the sail even though it was wet and beginning to get a little cold. Once under the bridge in West Bay, we could see the lodge off to port. The folks at the lodge were glad to see us. November is not primetime in Panama City, and we were the only boat at the dock. It's a good stop, comfortable, and has a good dining room for seafood. They took us in, and we relaxed in comparative luxury.

We had a meeting at breakfast. I opened the discussion. "The weather report is terrible. Winds out of the northwest at 20 to 25 knots with gusts possibly up to 40 knots. Small craft warnings are in effect. Small craft are advised to remain in inland waters. We are about eight miles from the marina and will have to close reach or tack most of the way. The last part will probably be the worst, since we may have to tack up Grand Lagoon, and it gets pretty narrow." Pat was having a big breakfast, and I hoped that his stomach would remain calm.

"Why don't we just use the motor and motor back?"

"I was planning on using the motor, but I don't think that the little outboard will push us into a twenty-knot wind, much less twenty-five or thirty. We are going to have to run the motor and sail and be uncomfortable. There won't be any danger unless the mast blows off and falls on someone's head, but it's going to take a while, and it's going to be wet. Or we could stay here all day if you want to." They both voted to go ahead, so we started getting ready. I called the marina and told the major to watch out for us, that I hoped to be off the Grand Lagoon by two or three o'clock. The Major is the dock master and a real nice guy. He said he would watch out for us and tow us in if we needed it.

We put up the storm sail, a small, loose-footed dingy sail that I attach to the main boom when the wind gets too strong. We took down the regular jib and put up a small jib I had once used on a Thistle sailboat. With this reduced sail, I figured we would not get knocked down and might even be able to sail some. We put on our foul-weather gear and at about 10:00 took off under sail and motor. We had no problem at all until after we cleared the bridge and hit the main bay. There we felt the full force of the wind, and a big puff knocked us over. The rail went under, and about ten gallons of water came in the cockpit. I didn't think we were going to founder, but there was a lot of water sloshing around. *Regardless* came back up and the water started out the scuppers, which fortunately were not clogged. My crew did fine and were not visibly upset. Pat began to bail with a plastic bucket and before long the cockpit was fairly clear.

"I plan to keep the motor going full blast and sail down toward the channel until we get opposite the entrance to Grand Lagoon. We should be able to do that without too much of a problem, but we'll have to keep the sails up, because I don't think the motor can do it without some help." The sail down the bay wasn't too bad. We didn't press *Regardless* hard and didn't experience any more knockdowns, although the rail was down most of the time. Maybe about one o'clock we were off the Lagoon entrance and, sure enough, the wind was coming straight at us.

"Now we have some work to do because the Lagoon is not very wide, and we are going to have to tack back and forth under sail and power. We should know pretty shortly whether we have a reasonable hope of getting back to the marina this afternoon."

We tacked toward Bay Point and seemed to be making some progress, and then tacked back toward St. Andrews Park. I figured we had gained about forty or fifty yards. Then back again toward Bay Point. On some tacks, I don't think we gained anything at all, while on some there would be a lull and we would make maybe a hundred yards or so. Ten, fifteen, twenty tacks (I didn't count them), and finally we could see the marina dock. I saw a small boat shove off and head toward us. It was the major in his outboard, bless his heart.

He came alongside. "I'm not sure I can tow you in this wind, but I can try if that's what you want."

"Major, I may be a little butt-headed, but I've brought the boat this far and I think I can dock it, but if you would please stand by in case we have a problem, I will certainly appreciate it.

"Go ahead, but wave something if you want me back," he said.

Another tack and still another, and we were finally getting close. "This may be it," I said, and headed in toward the dock. It didn't turn out that way. We missed the dock by about ten feet and had to tack out again. "This time we should be well above the marina dock and have no trouble, except we may be coming in a little fast." We tacked again and this time we were definitely going to make it, and it was going to be a fast landing; stopping a sailboat is sometimes a bigger problem than starting one. The major saw our problem and held up two bumpers which I assumed he was going to use to soften our collision.

"Rosser. Pat. This is going to be a little hairy," I said, "so I want you to do exactly what I tell you, when I tell you. We are now about fifty yards from the dock and coming in fast. When we are about twenty yards away, I want the jib down—promptly. And when we get about ten yards away, I want the main sail down, and it has to come down fast. The jib shouldn't be a problem. When I yell, pull it down, try to keep it out of the water. The main is going to be more of a problem because it won't come down by itself. You are going to have to yank the luff down, and it may take both of you. Okay. Here we go."

"Jib down, now!" I let go of the halyard and the jib came down and went straight into the water and under the boat. So much for seamanship. But it was an old jib, and it was slowing us down some. Fifteen yards away I hollered for the main, and this time they both yanked at the luff and down it came, exactly as I hoped it would. With no sails on and the motor in reverse, we nosed up to the dock, and the major grabbed our line. I was proud of myself and proud of my crew. Except that the jib was under the boat and probably fouled with the rudder, we had made a beautiful landing.

The major was standing on the dock, looking up at the rigging. I thought the least he could do would be to offer some congratulatory remarks upon our seamanship. Instead he kept looking up the mast and muttering something to himself. I think he said, "I don't think I've ever seen anything like that before." I looked up the mast, too, and there, hanging in the rigging, was our anchor. The anchor rod had fouled the main halyard, and the anchor had gone up as we pulled the sail down. The major said, "Don't worry, I'll get the boathook and we'll pull it down."

The guy in the next slip walked over. I had never liked him. He always wore a yachting cap and smoked a pipe. "Do you always carry the anchor that way?" he asked and smiled.

I tried to think of something clever to say, but there was that damn anchor hanging in the rigging. I thought maybe I ought to change crews. If I could find her, maybe Linda would like to go yachting on a boat.

"You guys straighten up a little bit and see if you can get the anchor down. I'm going to walk over to Captain Anderson's." Maybe her name wasn't Linda, but I knew what she looked like and I knew where she lived. There are some good women sailors, and after all, once aboard, the "captain's word is law."

Escape from Soddy Daisy

THERE REALLY IS A PLACE called Soddy Daisy. It sounds unlikely, but you can look it up if you have a big enough map. It's on the north side of Lake Chickamauga, maybe thirty miles from Chattanooga. I had been there once before, when, after a cocktail party in Chattanooga, my host, who was driving, was unable to locate his home on Missionary Ridge.

It was raining and dark, and when I saw a sign that said "Soddy Daisy City Limits, Population 293," I knew something was wrong. My host's wife saw the sign at the same time that I did and got a little upset. She insisted on driving home, which was just as well.

Now I was back in Soddy Daisy sitting with Piggy in our big outboard at the Soddy Daisy marina. We had not planned to come to Soddy Daisy and were anxious to leave as soon as possible.

It started out well enough when the Rome Power Squadron group arrived with eight boats at the Harrison Bay Marina. Piggy had his big outboard, and I helped Evelyn and two of the children aboard, along with our overnight things, picnic hamper, and ice chest full of beer. It took a while to get organized, but finally all eight boats were in the water, and we were getting ready to go downstream through the Chickamauga locks to spend the night at a motel near Hales Bar. I was looking forward to the trip, for this is probably the most beautiful section of the entire Tennessee Valley lakes. The river winds in a deep valley between Lookout Mountain and Signal Mountain, and the cliffs of Lookout Mountain seem to hang over the river and the banks are thickly forested.

Piggy's big Scott motor started without a problem, and we headed out to the channel to wait for the rest of the boats. Piggy always liked to be first, and when he gunned the motor we came out on a plane for a few seconds until the motor jumped out of gear. We tried it a couple more times—same thing. The motor would run fine in neutral, and okay at slow speeds, but jumped out of gear when we accelerated. We were sitting there with the motor idling when Billy Ledbetter came alongside to check on our problem.

We tried a couple more times, but the motor kept jumping out of gear, so after some talk with Billy and some of the other squadron members, we headed back to the dock. The marina operator told us that there was a Scott dealer at Soddy Daisy about ten miles up the lake, and Piggy called to see if he had an inventory of parts. He said he did, and after some more conversation, Evelyn and the children got in the boat with Billy and our gear (except for the beer, which I, with considerable foresight, kept with us). The rest of the squadron went on to the lock. Piggy and I would get the motor fixed and come on down later in the afternoon.

We headed upstream at a stately five or six miles per hour; I figured it would take at least two hours to get to the marina.

Piggy claimed he knew what was the matter, and had decided that a small spring in the lower unit had broken or gone bad. Piggy was an expert outboard mechanic and thought that he could fix our problem without undue difficulty.

It took us two hours, but we finally arrived at the Soddy Daisy Marina. About a mile off the river in a nice cove, it was an attractive marina with modern docks and what appeared to be a marine store and other boat facilities. We stopped at the gas dock. Piggy got out to investigate. It was a busy day, and we were a little in the way, so I moved the boat away from the gas pump and sat down to wait. It was hot, so after a while I walked up to a small stand at the end of the dock and looked over the menu. It was limited, but I was hungry and bought a moon pie and a Coke. I hoped we were not going to have a problem. Piggy finally reappeared and happily announced that everything was going to be fine. They were going to haul the boat for us, and Piggy would put in the new part. Sure enough, a young fellow arrived in a pickup truck hauling a sizable trailer, and before long our boat had been hauled up the ramp, and we were sitting in the parking lot. The truck departed, the young fellow assuring us that he would be back when we got the motor fixed.

I repeat that Piggy is an expert outboard mechanic and had a full set of tools aboard. We began to dismantle the lower unit, my job consisting principally of arranging the parts on old newspapers as Piggy removed them from the unit. There were more parts in that lower unit than I had expected, but Piggy appeared to know what he was doing and finally removed what was left of the lower unit itself and started taking it apart. Finally, he stood up and, with obvious satisfaction, held out to me a small spring which appeared to be in poor condition. "That's it," he said. "See how it's bent in the middle? It's not much of a part, but it keeps the motor in gear, and that was our problem. I can put this thing back together in thirty minutes, and we'll be off to Hales Bar." Piggy went off to get the new part and I wondered whether I ought to finish the rest of my moon pie. It was bought and paid for, so I finished it, although I questioned my judgment at the time.

Piggy was gone a good while, and when he finally got back it was obvious that something was wrong. "They don't have the part," he said. "That stupid son-of-a-bitch told me on the telephone that they had the part, and he told me again when I went up a while ago that he had it. Now he says he is sorry, that he was mistaken. The warehouse in Chattanooga is closed until Monday, and he says there is nothing he can do about it, that he is busy and short of help and that he is sorry."

What had been an inconvenience that we were bearing up under pretty well now became a serious problem. I said somewhat foolishly, ''Piggy, do you realize that we are a hundred miles from nowhere with no car and your motor scattered all over the parking lot?''

''I know, I know,'' he said, ''I started to hit the sonofabitch, but I promised Dot a while ago that I wouldn't do things like that anymore.'' He sat down on the trailer tire—it was obviously my turn. I had not hit anybody in a very long time and had always been afraid that if I did, they would probably hit me back. But I was mad as hell, so I walked up to the marina office looking for the operator. He was behind the counter, and there were a number of people in front of it. I waited impatiently, and finally he finished with his customers enough to want to know what I wanted. I tried to be pleasant, but it was difficult. ''I want to get back to Harrison Bay,'' I said, ''I am with Piggy Green, and we have his boat pulled in the lot with the motor torn into about forty-seven pieces, and now you tell us that you don't have the part we need.'' He was obviously uncomfortable, but that wasn't going to help us much. ''I'm sorry about the part,'' he said; ''we generally carry it, but there is really nothing I can do about it before Monday.''

''Just what are we supposed to do?'' I said. ''We depended on you, and now we are sitting out in the sun with no way to go anywhere. Can you rent us a boat to get back to Harrison Bay or get somebody to take us down there?''

''I'm sorry,'' he said, ''this is my busiest afternoon and I don't have much help. Maybe sometime later today I'll be able to help you, but not now.'' He turned to wait on another customer, and I was dismissed.

I walked back to the boat. Piggy was still sitting on the tire. I climbed up into the boat and sat down in a lawn chair I had brought from home. I called to Piggy, ''Come on up and get comfortable, something good may happen.'' He climbed into the boat and there we sat, two grown men sitting in an open outboard boat on a trailer in a parking lot with no motor and no automobile. I looked in the ice chest and noted with some satisfaction that there was a six-pack of beer on ice as well as a few soft drinks. I opened a beer. Piggy accepted a big orange or something like that. The beer was cold, and it didn't take me very long to finish the first can. Piggy hadn't said much since finding out about the parts except to make a few hostile noises. "Piggy," I said, "let's examine our alternatives. It is possible that there is a taxi in Soddy Daisy which would carry us to Harrison Bay for about fifty dollars or more. It is also possible that we may be able to pay somebody to carry us back by boat, although most of these people seem to be water-ski types. I could call home, but there is nobody there, and you say you have already tried to call Hugh."

Piggy mumbled something which seemed to have to do with the broken part. I opened another beer and walked down to the gas dock. Four young people came up in a ski boat, and I asked one of them about getting a ride to Harrison Bay.

"Sorry, neighbor," he said, "we're headed up river to Watts Bar, but I am sure somebody will come along."

I didn't share his confidence, but there wasn't much else to do, so I sat down on a Coca Cola crate and waited for the next customer. An old johnboat came up slowly, its sole occupant a no-longer-young fisherman. I took his line and tied him near the gas pump. He bought a few gallons of gas, and I asked him if he had had any luck fishing.

"Not a thing," he said, "just bounced up and down all day by these damn skiers, nearly got run over two or three times. They don't look where they are going and don't care. I might as well forget about the fish." He looked at my beer. It was a hot day and I figured he was thirsty.

"Neighbor," I said, "my friend and I are really needing a ride to Harrison Bay. Our motor is broken down and we've got no way to get back. You say you're not catching any fish, and we will gladly pay you to take us back."

"I don't know," he said, looking at the beer can.

"Would you like to have a beer?" I said. "I think I've got a couple more in the cooler."

"It is awful hot," he said, "and they don't sell beer in Soddy Daisy."

"I'll be right back," I said. Piggy was still sitting in the boat. "Hand me that cooler, I think I may have something going," and I opened a beer and brought it to my new friend. He wasted no time and seemed appreciative. I didn't rush him, and we sat together like old friends, drinking our beer. Finally I said, "We'll give you five dollars and I'll throw in my last beer. Just take us down to Harrison Bay and leave us at the dock." He thought it about it for a while, but finally said, "Okay, but you might get me the beer now."

We had our clothes in Ledbetter's boat, so the only thing we had was the ice chest. Piggy had the parts back in the boat, and we were nearly ready to go. "Tell the damn operator we'll be back for the boat, no thanks to him, and I'll give our friend another beer," I said. Piggy appeared at the dock with the ice chest, and we were ready to go.

My new friend looked at Piggy somewhat dubiously and said, "Gosh, he's big. I'm not sure we can get him in the boat. How would it be if I just took you and you came back after him?"

"That won't work at all," I said. "He's not that fat, and we will be fine." I wasn't sure how fine we would be, but we all got in the boat. I figured we had about three or four inches of freeboard, which might be enough if we didn't hit any big waves. The boat had a seven- or eight-horsepower motor, and we weren't going to go anywhere very fast. I waited until we got away from the dock before I started looking for the bailing can. There was one, and I figured we'd need it.

It was getting late in the afternoon and the traffic had died down some, but there was still a good bit of chop out in the lake. Occasionally some water came aboard, but I managed to stay ahead of it—just barely. My new friend said, "I told you he was

too big. Maybe we ought to take him back. I'm not sure we can make it to Harrison Bay.''

"We'll be fine," I said. "I can keep the water out, and besides, I think I have another beer in the ice chest." I opened the last beer and gave it to him. The argument was settled, at least for the time being. Our host grumbled from time to time, but I kept bailing when necessary, and he finally deposited us on the dock at Harrison Bay. He was looking a little groggy, and I hoped he would make it back. We shook hands and he started back out the channel. It was getting a little dark, and I noticed he didn't have any running lights. Maybe he didn't live far up the river.

We waved our goodbyes and started looking for our truck.

We were very late getting to the motel at Hales Bar. It had been a very busy day. I called the marine patrol and told them we were safe and to call off the search. There was a small bottle of bourbon in my clothes bag. I took off the top and handed it to Piggy. We poured drinks in paper cups. I held mine up to him—"Another successful cruise." Piggy gulped and coughed. I thought he said something about a broken spring.

Starboard, Dammit!

When two yachts on opposite tacks are sailing converging courses, the yacht on the starboard tack shall have the right of way and the port tack yacht shall give way and stay clear. A violation by the port tack yacht shall result in disqualification.

RULES OF UNITED STATES
YACHT RACING UNION

G.L. WAS AT THE tiller of his newly acquired Y-Flyer, and I was sailing as crew and instructor. G.L. was determined to sail in the Y-Flyer Southeastern Regatta, although he had practically no sailing experience and I had very little in the Y-Flyer class. It was Saturday morning, and a nice day. The wind was light but fairly steady from the southwest. I counted twenty-six boats. This was a big regatta for Allatoona, and there were lots of out-of-town entries.

We jockeyed around in the general area of the start, but tried to stay clear of the boats we thought were the principal competitors.

"G.L., all the hot skippers will be crowding the windward end of the line and getting in each other's way. Why don't we start somewhere along the middle and keep out of the heavy traffic?"

"Okay, okay," he said.

I heard the ten-minute gun go off and saw the white flag flying on the committee boat. There would be a five-minute gun and a blue flag before the start. The blue flag comes down exactly one minute before the start, and there is a lot of hectic maneuvering before the starting gun.

Sailboat races start exactly on time. When I used to race a good bit, I had a stopwatch that we started at the five-minute gun. The perfect start is to hit the line under full sail and with good speed at the instant the gun sounds. If you are over too soon, you have to go back and start again, which is disastrous. If you are too far back, you can pretty well forget it and concentrate on enjoying the sail.

We sort of sat behind the line and tried to stay out of the way, but when the gun fired we made a fairly good start and headed in the general direction of the weather mark, which was about a mile away. It was going to be a beat with lots of tacks, which is what the race committee wanted.

I don't know where he came from. Most of the fleet was to windward and ahead. We had gone over to a port tack to try to get upwind a little ourselves, when here he came, straight at us. Number 3033. I remember it well, and I particularly remember the skipper, who had a thick shock of gray hair and a pipe in his mouth. He was on a starboard tack and closing fast. "G.L.," I said, "I don't think we can clear him. You are going to have to decide what to do." G.L.'s hand was steady on the tiller and his eyes were steady, staring straight ahead toward the weather mark.

3033 was getting a good puff of wind, and I figured he would probably hit us about amidships. He was close now, and I could see his jaw was set on his pipe. Now we were real close—he took the pipe out of his mouth, stood up, and hollered, "Starboard! Starboard, dammit!"

G.L.'s hand was steady on the tiller, and we did not waiver from our course. 3033 came about suddenly, and we sailed on. I thought I heard "Starboard!" again, but I'm not sure. I looked

back at 3033 and saw that the crew was attaching a red handkerchief to the port shroud.

"G.L., we are being protested."

"What?" he said, beginning to regain consciousness. "How do you know?"

"Don't look now, but there is a red flag in the rigging of 3033 and it wasn't there a minute ago."

G.L. and I are both lawyers and I was not surprised when he said, "Frankly, I need to study these racing rules more carefully. Exactly what is our legal position?"

"I am not an expert on the rules either, but the starboard-tack boat has the right of way and the red flag means that he is going to file a protest against us. When the race is over, he will have to serve us with a written protest and we will all get a chance to testify before the race committee. If they rule against us, we will be disqualified."

G.L. said, "That seems like an awful lot of doing about a small matter. Have you ever been involved in a protest before?"

"Yes, I have been protested three times, and I have lost every single one of them. I appeared once with witnesses but still lost. I considered appealing to the committee on appeals in New Orleans, but decided that I was being childish. You have to remember that these people are extremely competitive and that this is a serious business among serious competitors. That guy may have driven 500 miles to this regatta, and we certainly didn't do him any good."

Our attention had been diverted, and I again noticed that most of the fleet was now well ahead. "Let's concentrate on sailing the boat and see if we can beat somebody." At the windward mark, we were clearly ahead of three boats. One was having halyard trouble, and the main sail had come about halfway down the mast. The other two boats seemed to be sailed by teenagers, and the crew of one was dragging her feet in the water. 3033 must have gotten himself straightened out, for I thought I saw a boat up ahead flying a red flag. We rounded the mark and set off on the second leg. The race was set for two laps around a triangular course; the finish line would be near the club docks. The wind was still fairly steady, but the other boats seemed to be getting farther and farther away. On the third leg, the leader lapped us, and pretty soon so did most of the fleet. 3033 was in pretty good position about the middle of the fleet. He did not look our way when he passed, but was still flying the protest flag. The boat with the jammed halyard apparently had been towed back to the club, and the teenagers had disappeared. We were definitely in possession of last place.

About halfway through the second lap things began to get pretty lonely; to add to our problems, the breeze, which had been light but steady, began to drop. When we finally rounded the last mark, it was getting dusky dark, and we couldn't see any other boats. We kept moving slowly and began to look for the finish line. The lights in the clubhouse came on—the cocktail party would be starting pretty soon. We never did find the finish line. The committee had taken it up and gone home.

We sat at the dock; G.L. seemed deep in thought. I took down the sails and put them in the bag, and he still just sat there. "Come on, G.L., we have to go to the protest hearing and defend ourselves," I said.

"Oh, that," he said. "Do you think they will still have it?"

"I'm not sure, but I have to go to the restroom anyway, so let's go on up to the clubhouse."

The cocktail party was getting underway when we came in. Fred P. saw me come in and came over. "Where have you guys been?" he said. "The race committee has been looking for you about a protest. I think by now they must have posted you as DNF," Did Not Finish. The results were already on the bulletin board. We were there all right, but with no comment. I told G.L. that we could demand to be disqualified or something. This business of ignoring us was humiliating.

G.L. said, "I'm tired. I think I would like for us to go on home if you don't mind." When we went out the door, the skipper of

3033 was coming in. He looked sharp in a turtleneck sweater and was puffing on his pipe. If he recognized us, he didn't speak. G.L. called me that night and said that he wasn't feeling too well and would I mind if we didn't sail the Sunday races. I didn't mind at all, and I thought that old 3033 would be happy to know that we were not on the course. The next week I went down with G.L., and we hauled his boat and carried it home. I'm not sure what happened to it. There is, however, a good market for used sailboats in the Atlanta area.

Off the Coast of Maine

MALABAR XIV was waiting for us at the dock in Camden, Maine. She had been there several weeks since Harvey competed in the New York Yacht Club cruise and races, and it was to be our job to sail her to Newport, Rhode Island. *Malabar XIV* is a namesake of the famous *Malabar* designed and built by John Alden, who first demonstrated the feasibility of taking small sailing crafts offshore for extended periods of time. *Malabar XIV* was built by the Alden yard at Newport, Rhode Island, and is a fifty-five-foot ketch with over 10,000 pounds of lead, ballast, and keel. She had only recently been completed, and this was her second sea trial.

We committed our first tactical error when we let the taxi go at the Camden Marina. We had no supplies on board except some nearly empty whiskey bottles, and it was at least half a mile back to town. Camden is a small, pretty town on a pretty harbor featuring freshly painted buildings and looking much like most of the small, attractive towns in Maine. Our skipper prepared a list of supplies needed for the seven-day cruise, and we went off on foot. Unfortunately, we had made a second miscalculation, for there is not much in Camden, Maine, to begin with, and nothing was open on the Saturday night before Labor Day. That is, nothing much. We finally found a convenience store where we were able to buy a few basic groceries. We did find a good seafood restaurant with a bar, so all was not lost. We spent the night tied to the dock; it would be the last dock we tied to until we got to Newport.

SUNDAY

I have done a good bit of cruising and have always been pretty relaxed about my itinerary. Our skipper, Harvey, was apparently even more relaxed, for when we left the dock nobody seemed to know exactly where we were going except that it was south. We had a late start due to another effort to get additional supplies. We took a turn around the harbor before heading out under power. It was a beautiful, sunshiny day with a light wind from the east. The coast is rocky, and the water very deep, except, of course, where the rocks stick out or come close to sticking out of the water. There is no inland waterway, so when you go out, you are out. This Sunday it was calm and beautiful, and after a while we put up the sails and eased along at a stately two or three knots.

Around four or five o'clock we began to look for a place to spend the night. For no particular reason we came into Tenants Harbor, a beautiful small harbor with a deep-water anchorage and no observable village. There were pretty white houses lining the shore, and we made out a particularly large one which looked like it might be an inn. The anchor went down in about eighty feet of water, and after some maneuvering our skipper declared we were safe for the night. Anchoring *Malabar XIV* consists of letting out a considerable length of very heavy chain operated by a power windlass at the bow; the anchor and chain are far too heavy to be handled manually. The anchor securely down, it was time to worry about the dinghy. A beautiful Dyer ten-foot dinghy was strapped down on the deck. Unfortunately, Mr. John

107

Alden had not yet worked out the details of getting it overboard and back again. The method of launching consisted of getting the dinghy in an upright position on the deck without scratching the brightwork, attaching it by a complicated series of swings through blocks on the main boom. The boom was then swung out, and the dinghy lowered using the main halyard on a big winch. As far as I am concerned, this is a feature that needs to go back to the drawing board. After about thirty or forty minutes of combined efforts by the crew of four, the dinghy was finally overboard and floating.

The harbor was beautiful and the weather was good, so we got ready to go ashore. Harvey decided that the dinghy could not safely carry all four of us, so our first mate, Steve, rowed the other guest, Robert, in first. It was Sunday, so Steve, Harvey, and I, complete with jackets and ties, rowed up to the inn dock. It was a nice inn, more or less typical of many country inns in Maine. Sunday dinner was apparently very popular, so we spent thirty or forty minutes in rocking chairs on a wide porch overlooking the harbor having mixed drinks, served somewhat secretively in deference to local law.

Dinner was an outstanding seafood feast, and we took our time. When we were ready to go back to the boat, it appeared that, under the influence of several drinks, the dinghy had now become safe for all four of us. So, carrying a freeboard of three or four inches, we made our way back aboard without incident.

MONDAY

Our skipper was not an early riser, so we seldom got under way before ten o'clock. Neither Robert nor I had any idea how far it was to Newport, but we knew we wanted to get there by Saturday. Harvey declared that we were ahead of schedule, and that we would spend the day exploring the Maine coast. The Maine Coast is certainly worth exploring. There are thousands of islands, some simply bare rocks and others having a few trees or an occasional house. There are also many small villages where the only industry is lobster fishing and tourism. Mostly under motor, we went close in to Fort Clyde and then to Friendship, the home of the famous Friendship sloop. We went around island after island enjoying the scenery and beautiful weather. The dinghy was in tow and gave no trouble in the calm water.

Harvey and Steve agreed that Booth Bay would be a good overnight stop. After a good bit more motoring, we headed into Booth Bay Harbor. Booth Bay is an extensive town by Maine standards, and the harbor was crowded with anchored boats. The main sail was up and the motor turning slowly as we began to look for an anchorage. There are no transient docks or slips in Maine, but some of the more popular harbors furnish guest moorings that can be rented.

We were looking for a guest mooring when the motor quit. I was at the wheel, and Steve was getting the anchor ready. Harvey was somewhat upset about being in a crowded anchorage with no motor. I asked whether the boat would tack under main sail alone, and he said he thought so. We certainly could jibe if we had to. Harvey gave his attention to the motor, and I jibed without difficulty. The wind was a steady ten knots. I figured we could jibe back and forth for a long time if necessary. We did. One drawback to motors on sailboats is that you absolutely cannot depend on them working when needed. A sailor who has to have a motor to get back to the slip had better take up some other hobby. After two or three jibes, the motor started, and the harbormaster directed us to a guest mooring not far from a public landing.

I liked Booth Bay. It is a sizable town of pretty homes, clean pleasant shops, and a pretty, crowded harbor. There were signs that the merchants were getting ready for the tourists to leave, and I guess it is pretty deserted by November. I did some shopping, made a phone call to be certain that the Coast Guard had not been alerted, had another good seafood dinner, then went back to the boat and went to bed.

TUESDAY

We got another late start and decided that it was time to stow the dinghy. This operation, again requiring the combined efforts of four men, was neatly accomplished in approximately forty-five minutes. You have to have a dinghy in New England, and the Dyer is very pretty; however, an inflatable snugged up to the stern would be a lot less trouble.

We cleared Booth Bay Harbor in a light overcast and with a good fifteen-knot breeze on the port quarter. The boat was not easy to steer with quartering waves of two to three feet, and it took a lot of doing to keep within about five compass points of our course. We did make good progress, however, sometimes running up as much as seven or eight knots on the meter. Soon the overcast had burned away, and for a good many hours it was the kind of sailing day sailors dream of—off shore on a broad reach in the sunshine.

We were nearing Portland and decided that there was no particular reason to go into the harbor. Harvey knew of a small cove behind an island not far from Portland, so with the wind on the stern and dropping, we ghosted up to a mooring someone had kindly provided and tied up without even bothering to start the motor. Harvey took charge of the galley and prepared a complicated and delicious fish chowder. It had been a fairly long day, so, after a half-hearted attempt at Scrabble, we went to bed.

Harvey and I slept late, but Steve not only had the coffee ready, but the anchor ready to come up when we finally arose. Later Steve also cooked breakfast and made life comfortable for us in general.

Here I shall say a word about our crew. Harvey Howalt is a businessman from Dalton, Georgia, and a very experienced sailor. Some years ago, he purchased Prince Rainier's eighty-foot yacht, and, with a crew of friends, sailed it across the Atlantic to Barbados and then up to Florida. He is a member of the New York Yacht Club and a part owner of the John Alden Boat Yard. He is an experienced ocean racer, and also owns and races a J-24 out of the Privateer Yacht Club in Chattanooga. You can be comfortable with Harvey at the helm.

Steve Tibbets, also from Dalton, is a professional chemist. Steve was born in Maine not far from Camden, but has been in the South long enough not to want to go back except on visits. Steve is the kind of crewman every skipper would like to have— agile, knowledgeable, and always ready for the task at hand. Steve not only handled most of the chores in the galley, but also handled the anchor and spent hours at the helm. Steve can go with me anytime.

Robert Davison, another businessman from Dalton, is an attractive, pleasant sailing companion. Robert knows nothing about sailing, and is not a fast learner. However he was always willing to help in every situation.

As for me, I am long on small-boat sailing experience but weak on electronics and mechanics, both of which I mistrust thoroughly. I never had anything more complicated than a compass on any of my boats until a few years ago, and sometimes even the compass didn't work. I am also getting a little slow in the agility department, which makes me a less-than-desirable crew on an off-shore cruise.

WEDNESDAY

We got the anchor up—or at least Steve and the winch got it up—and we motored around our island and through Portland Harbor. It was misty and the visibility was restricted. The weather report was for northerly winds from twenty to twenty-five knots and possibly light rain. "This is the day we head south," Harvey announced, and under full main and genoa we headed to sea. The wind had picked up to about twenty knots, and it was uncomfortably cold. I put on my heavy underwear, sweater, jacket, and ski cap, and later a full suit of foul-weather gear. We were on a broad reach with the wind on the port quarter, and the boat was very difficult to hold on any reasonable compass course. Everyone overestimates the height of waves, but these were big ones, six to eight feet—not breaking, but lifting the quarter as they went under the stern. Under these conditions, the idea is to bring the boat up slightly into the wave and then ride off. It is not easy to do, and as the boat comes off the wave, there is the danger of an involuntary jibe. We took turns at the wheel, which was not fun to handle. After a few hours, I went below with the idea of taking a nap, but the movement of the boat was so pronounced that I began to feel I could be seasick. I have never been seasick, but this might be the first time, so I stayed on deck and suffered along with everybody else.

I did go below long enough to look at the Loran. While I distrust all instruments, I was fascinated with the Loran, which furnished a continuous longitude and latitude reading. It was a simple matter to plot a position at any time, and according to my reckoning, we were now over twenty miles off shore, well out of sight of land. Sometime during the afternoon, when Robert was at the wheel, a particularly big wave caused him to lose control, and we suffered a vicious jibe. Harvey, who had been below reading, came on deck, and we managed to come over so that we could resume reaching on the port tack. Harvey gave Robert some words of advice and took the helm. Sometime later, Robert was restored to grace and took the helm again—unfortunately, with the same result. A jibe under these conditions is particularly dangerous and can carry away the mast or break any part of the rigging. Robert was again demoted, but unfortunately, not permanently. I suggested to Harvey that I would feel more comfortable with a ''preventer,'' but, for some reason, we did not rig it.

By five o'clock conditions had not improved, and Robert had been restored to the helm. I had gone below to see if my stomach was in any better condition when we jibed for the third time. The boom came over with a vicious snap, making a noise like a rifle shot, and Steve hollered that something had broken. Harvey and I came on deck to see the main boom completely out of control and whipping viciously back and forth. The main block on the traveler had broken in two from the force of the jibe, and the block was sailing around wildly and likely to do serious bodily harm. I tried to get it under control, but after seeing it whiz by my head, I decided that there must be a better way. We started the motor and were able to round up into the wind and get a temporary line over the end of the boom. It is possible that we could have sailed under this rig, but conditions seemed to be getting worse, and we started towards Portsmouth under power. Things were very uncomfortable, but certainly not dangerous.

There must be hundreds of lighthouses in Maine. I had never before thought of a lighthouse as having anything to do with me personally. Some of them are painted with stripes and look pretty on postcards. We, of course, knew that they were navigational aids, said to be very helpful to the sailor. It was beginning to get dark, and we were still some eight or ten miles offshore but closing fairly fast. The weather was very bad, and we were closing on a rocky coast. Harvey turned on the radar, which, according to him, showed that we were on course for the Portsmouth channel and should see the strobe on the lighthouse before long. The radar was all very well and of some comfort; Harvey had confidence in the radar and the Loran, but all four of us were anxiously eyeing the horizon for the lighthouse that was supposed to show up off the starboard bow. To our relief, the light finally showed up about where we expected it, but there was no lighthouse. The strobe light seemed disembodied in the mist, but was easily identifiable, and a while later we saw the actual lighthouse.

With the lighthouse in view, we crept up the channel into Portsmouth Harbor. It was getting dark when we spotted some other sailboats at anchor, so Steve let ours go, and it was time for the cocktail hour. After two drinks, Robert conceded that he had

been very concerned about our situation, and in addition to having jibed three times, he had been seasick and in general had had a miserable day. My day hadn't been all that bad, but I was glad to be at anchor. I confessed to Robert that my secret for not jibing accidentally was to sail about ten degrees off course, with the wind more on the beam; this caused Steve to comment that the way I was sailing the boat, we were heading toward the Azores.

We had a quiet night, and Harvey announced that if we really intended to get to Newport by Saturday, we had a long trip ahead of us.

THURSDAY

We had the anchor up fairly early and were headed south toward the Cape Cod Canal. It was probably our best sailing day, although it was very, very long. The wind was now mostly on the port beam, and the waves were down to three or four feet.

We were soon out of sight of land again, but the sun was out and the sky was fairly clear so we were not concerned. The boat was much easier to steer now and our improvised traveler seemed to work even better than the original model. We were too far off-shore to see Boston, but were able to spot the pilgrim's monument at Provencetown on the tip of Cape Cod. We made a steady seven to nine knots for about ten hours, then decided to go into Plymouth, which we thought would leave us not too long a day to Newport.

It was beginning to get dark as we entered Plymouth Harbor. The entry to the harbor is fairly complicated but well marked. There are some ugly shoals on either side of the channel, but we finally arrived at the inner harbor without difficulty. The harbor-master passed us in his boat—presumably off duty and going home. We hailed him, and he advised us that there were guest moorings available at the yacht club. We were able to get the yacht club on the radio, and their tender came out and directed us to a mooring. Unfortunately, he was about to go off duty too, so there would be no shore dinner that night. Plymouth Harbor is a quaint, attractive place—very sheltered, making you wonder how the pilgrims ever found it in the first place, unless the shoals and bars were very differently located in those days. Steve and Harvey concocted a stew of beef and beans; after the long day it tasted good.

Robert and I cleaned the galley. I proposed to sleep on deck, but it was uncomfortably cold. Robert was anxious to get ashore to take a walk and do some last-minute shopping, so he had arranged for the yacht club launch to pick us up at 8:30 on Friday morning. By then we had not been ashore for three days, and I was anxious to take a walk myself. Even a 55-foot boat can get cramped, and there are very limited opportunities for any exercise except pulling lines and cranking windows. Harvey tried to teach us a poker game played with dice, but I showed no aptitude and went to bed early.

FRIDAY

The launch came bright and early and deposited Robert and me at the yacht club dock. The yacht club is a very attractive three-story building looking out on the harbor and apparently having its own moorings for members and guests. Robert took off for town, a short distance away, while I looked around the club and talked to a very attractive lady who seemed to be in charge. I told her of our sailing club in Rome and asked if I could purchase one of their burgees (sailing club flags) to display in our new club room. She graciously presented me with their burgee, which has an attractive red background with white stars. I promised to send her one of our burgees, which I did.

I wandered into town, trying out my land legs, which did not work too well. The town is very clean and attractive and was not too crowded with tourists. I wobbled along as far as Plymouth Rock, which proved to be a rather undistinguished gray rock lying on the beach and covered by a fairly elaborate building with concrete columns. It is located so that the tide comes in through an open grill and, I assume, covers the rock from time to time. Any reasonable size rock would serve the same purpose. Shortly past the rock I came to the replica of the Mayflower, which is tied to a dock and open for inspection by tourists. I would have liked to go aboard, but I had promised to be back by 10:00.

The launch carried me back to the boat where Harvey and Steve were obviously ready to get underway. I didn't know how far it was to Newport, but apparently they did.

It took a while to get out of the harbor against a fast-running tide, but a weather check indicated that we would have a favorable tide through the Cape Cod Canal, which is very important to sailboats.

It was a pretty slow morning with a light breeze, and we proceeded south under both sail and power, making about seven knots. The weather was beautiful, and when we reached the canal, the shores were lined with people picnicking and sunbathing; no one actually goes near the water, however, for it is far too cold for comfort. There was not much traffic on the canal, and we enjoyed the remainder of the beef stew while sitting at the cockpit table like a bunch of houseboaters.

We cleared the canal under motor in the early afternoon, and headed south down Buzzard's Bay with the islands of western Cape Cod on our left. Their names were Pasque, Nashawena, and Cuttyhunk, and reminded me of my days in the Power Squadron plotting courses on a training chart that just happened to be an actual chart of this area.

The wind, which had been very light and from the east, picked up considerably as we passed Cuttyhunk and went to the south. This suited us fairly well. Actually, except for Robert's involuntary jibes, we had been on a port tack for the last four days. The wind continued to build, and by mid-afternoon we were roaring along on a beam reach, registering about nine and a half knots most of the time, with the meter touching ten occasionally.

Several hours later I began to wonder how much farther it was to Newport, but a quick check of the Loran showed that it was still a long way off. I began to regret my stay in Plymouth that morning. This had been America's Cup territory until the Australians took the cup away, and we were having better winds than some of the America's Cup races enjoyed; I was looking forward to seeing the Brenton Reef light, long a landmark for the Cup races. Finally it began to get dark and we could see the lights onshore come on some five or six miles away. We had left Plymouth shortly after 10:00 A.M.; it was now 7:30 P.M., and still no Brenton Reef light. When it finally came into view, it was something of a disappointment, for it was difficult to pick out against the neon background of Newport Harbor. I liked the solitary Maine lighthouses much better.

This was the time for Harvey to get busy and get us into a crowded Newport Harbor. He turned on all the electronics and with the harbor chart in front of him began to shout directions to Steve, who had the helm. Robert and I tried to help by identifying various lights and navigational aids. Frankly, the skipper needed all the help he could get, particularly with respect to other boats in the vicinity.

It was 10:00 P.M. when we finally dropped anchor in what looked to be a likely spot. The dark harbor was crowded, it being the weekend of the sailboat show. Unfortunately, about the time we had declared cocktail time, the harbormaster's launch arrived and informed us that we had anchored in the channel and would have to move. He was not very helpful about where we would go; the burden of his message was, more or less, "just move." Steve got the anchor up again, and we began to motor around in the harbor looking for a place to stop. We finally found a place that looked likely, and this time we got no complaint from the harbormaster.

It was 10:30 P.M., and I was ready to have some corn flakes and go to bed. My shipmates, only slightly younger than I, had other ideas, however, and had already radioed for the launch to pick us up. I seriously considered defecting, but decided that it would be unseemly on our last night, so we donned our foul-weather suits, because it was beginning to drizzle. After a reasonable time, the launch arrived—a big, open boat that would hold twenty-five to thirty people. Apparently, the launch service in Newport circles the harbor more or less continuously, picking up people and taking others back to their boats. The launch was crowded, and its immediate mission was to carry a lady back to her boat. Unfortunately, she had forgotten its exact location, so we spent about twenty minutes cruising about the harbor looking at boat transoms with the tender operator's flashlight. I was beginning to wish I was practically anywhere else when the boat was finally found and the lady deposited on board. The launch then headed for the restaurant dock.

It was a good restaurant, and after another drink and some hot chowder I was almost glad I came. I was not glad for long, however, because when we got back to the dock at about 12:15 A.M. we were advised that the launch would not make its final run until 1:00, and if we expected to get back to our boat, we would have to be on it. I sat down on the wet dock and would have cried if I had not been a strong grown man. The launch did finally come, and we did finally find our boat, and I did finally get into my bunk, although it was well, well past my bedtime.

SATURDAY

We were up fairly early and headed up Narragansett Bay. The Alden boatyard is located at Milton, about ten miles up the bay, and by mid-morning we were tied to a dock and getting our belongings ready for the trip home.

We had had mostly great weather, but some bad; mostly good wind and some a little too good; some big waves and some little waves. We had seen some beautiful country and had been treated hospitably and fed well. We had not suffered any real hardship or real danger and had enjoyed some beautiful sailing. Nobody had gotten mad at anybody else, and it had been a great cruise. It was now time to go home and look at the pictures and tell friends about sailing off the New England coast.

"I Was in the Channel"

I CALLED THE P-G Welding and Marine Service. Hugh answered; he recognized my voice. "Dad's with a customer, but I doubt if he sells anything. They are probably just talking about boats and telling tales. Can I get him to call you?"

"Tell him that the Power Squadron is going to Watts Bar Saturday and that we'll spend the night at Pete Smith's Resort and come back sometime Sunday. If he will furnish the boat and motor and trailer, I will be glad to go."

"I think he is ready to go. We just got in a big outboard with a big motor and he's dying to try it out. Claims we're going to use it as a demonstrator. I bet the thing will go nearly fifty miles an hour, and if you go to Watts Bar, I'll guarantee you it'll run as fast as it can run all the way."

"I don't particularly mind fast. Hugh, why don't you go with us?"

"I wouldn't go anywhere with you old farts. You got too bad a record. I've had to come after you twice, and if you go this time, I'm going off somewhere or at least take my phone off the hook. You'll have to be rescued by somebody else."

"Hugh, you do realize that your father is an expert outboard motor mechanic, a former motorboat racer, and a master welder; and I am the educational officer of the Rome Power Squadron and spend a good bit of my spare time teaching classes on seamanship and safe boating."

"I've got no problem with your credentials, but I'm not going, and I doubt if you get anybody else to go with you. Good luck."

Saturday morning early I was at Piggy's shop admiring the boat. It was a big, pretty outboard with a nice cuddy topped by a navigation light and flagpole. The trailer was already hitched to the P-G Special, a truck whose ancestry included more than one motor and numerous parts from other vehicles.

There is a nice marina and launching ramp at Harrison Bay, a state park on Lake Chickamauga near Chattanooga. It's about sixty miles upstream to the lock and dam at Watts Bar. The Tennessee Valley lakes are among the most beautiful in the world, and Lake Chickamauga and the lake at Watts Bar are among the more beautiful. The lake is relatively undeveloped and lies in an area that is not densely populated. It's my choice of all of the Tennessee Valley lakes—wide, deep, and with a good many small islands. The river is navigable to Knoxville, but there is not a lot of barge traffic above Chattanooga.

The Rome Power Squadron, in addition to carrying on an active educational program, gets together several times a year for boat trips. The annual trip to Watts Bar has always been one of my favorites. This year we had nine boats and maybe thirty-five people. While we were waiting at the launching ramp, I found a small yacht ensign in the marina store. I attached it to the flagpole and felt that we were now ready to lead the fleet. We were not really supposed to lead the fleet; it would proceed at a moderate speed to accommodate the slower boats. However, I knew that once we cleared Harrison Bay we would open the throttle. Piggy takes the position that an outboard motor is supposed to run at full speed all of the time and that it is bad for the motor to run at anything less than full speed. This is not my field; I hate all motors and consider them all unreliable. I will take a canoe or sailboat anytime.

We stayed in formation until we cleared the last channel mark, and then we were off. We weren't carrying anything except our fuel and a small ice chest, so we must have been doing at least forty or forty-five miles an hour. Piggy doesn't believe in slowing down for waves or things like that, so I braced myself in the corner of the cockpit and held on. It was a fast trip.

The lock was open at Watts Bar and we went on through. By early afternoon we were at the dock at Pete Smith's with nothing much to do except watch the football game. Piggy suggested that we ride on up the lake, but I had had enough of outboarding for the time being.

Pete Smith's Watts Bar Resort occupies what was a village of temporary houses and buildings used by the workers during the construction of the dam and lock. I am not familiar with the business arrangement, but apparently the Tennessee Valley Authority leases the village to Pete, and he and his family have made it into an attractive place. There is a nice restaurant, swimming pool, lots of flowers, and the little cottages scattered over the property are well maintained. It's maybe half a mile from the docks, but Pete furnishes transportation back and forth on a regular basis.

I'm not sure when the rest of the Squadron arrived, but it was later. We would see them all at dinner. Maybe there would be a small cocktail party, but absolutely no speeches.

Pete will tolerate a small cocktail party in one of the cabins, but it is a dry county and he is careful about alcohol. No drinking and no bottles in the dining room, and none at the swimming pool if he knows about it. The cocktail party didn't materialize, so we decided to walk on up to the restaurant for dinner. I wrapped my pint bottle in my jacket and carried it along just in case. I didn't want to get crossways with Pete, so I stuck the bottle under a bush by the swimming pool and we went on in.

The dining room was full with our group and other people. "Piggy," I said, "there's a table over in the corner with a lady who seems to be by herself. Maybe she'll let us sit down." We walked over and she said she would be glad to have us. She was a nice-looking lady, neither old nor young, and she did look lonesome.

"I'm a little lonesome," she said. "My friend didn't make it, so I guess I'm stuck up here for the weekend."

"Maybe it won't be so bad," I said. "We're by ourselves. We could take you for a boat ride. It's a big lake and we have a big boat and plenty of fuel. Not tonight, though. Maybe tomorrow if the weather is pretty. I thought I saw a little sailboat at the dock. Maybe they'll rent it to us. I'd rather sail than bounce around in a motorboat anyway."

Piggy, who had been reading the menu with approval, said, "Yeah. You've been promising to teach me to sail. This might be a good chance. At least we can see if the boat is for rent."

Our lady was still looking at the menu, and nobody was paying us the slightest attention. I decided that it was time for a drink— I could step outside, retrieve my bottle, pour a little in my water glass, and return without undue commotion. I wondered if our lady would like to join me.

"This is a dry county," I said, "and Pete doesn't allow any alcohol in the dining room. However, I am about to go outside and pour a small drink into my water glass. If you would like to join me, I don't think we will cause a problem." She picked up her water glass, which was half-full of ice, and said, "Lead the way."

I led the way and we poured drinks out of my bottle, which I replaced under the bush. I didn't figure Pete was going to smell our water glasses, so we went back to the table. Service was slow and we had time to replenish our drinks before the food arrived. Piggy doesn't drink anymore. His wife, Dot, said it made him mean and she made him quit. I can't imagine Piggy being mean, but he doesn't take a drink, and I don't interfere with other people's habits unless they interfere with mine. I think non-drinking is a delightful habit for people who will drive the car or drive the boat and things like that.

Piggy stayed for dessert and camaraderie, but I suggested to our new friend that maybe we should have a drink by the pool. We sat and relaxed like old friends sometimes do. She wasn't anxious to talk, which suited me fine. It was dark now, and I felt fairly mellow. "Do we do names and things like that?" I said.

"I don't know," she said. "I think not. Maybe first names. I'm Marsha. That's enough."

"I'm Dudley." It was dark, and I felt like she smiled.

"Uncle Dudley," she said. "Wasn't there a character somewhere with that name? A gentle, nice, scoutmaster type?"

"Me exactly. A sweet, nice, thoughtful fellow, and I once did have a scout troop, but that was a long time ago."

"I think maybe you are a nice, sweet man. I'm not a nice, sweet woman. I'm mean and difficult and getting worse. I've had one ugly divorce and I'm fixing to have another one. Just came up here to think about it. He's really a pretty nice guy, but I want out. I really want out bad."

We just sat and sipped on our drinks for a while, and finally they were gone. "Marsha, I figure there are two more drinks in that bottle. Hand me your glass and we'll finish it off."

"Uncle Dudley, you told me you were a nice, sweet man and now you've about got me drunk. I don't need another drink. As it is, you may have to put me to bed."

She handed me her glass and I fixed the last two drinks. "I'm getting a little woozy myself, but I believe I can handle putting you to bed if you'll cooperate."

"Well now, Uncle Dudley, I don't know. Let's finish this last drink and I'll think about it. I am lonesome."

&

Piggy must have gotten up early. I opened my eyes at least part of the way and considered whether I ought to try to get up. I generally don't have headaches, but this was going to be an exception.

Piggy didn't quite bounce in, but he seemed unnecessarily cheerful. "I brought you hot coffee and donuts, and I have rented us the sailboat. It will be ready in about an hour. Drink some coffee and you may feel better."

Marsha's cabin was next door. I filled a coffee cup and went over and knocked. Nothing happened and I knocked again. "For God's sake, go away, whoever you are. Don't knock on that door again."

"Marsha, it's Dudley. I brought you some hot coffee. Open the door at least a little and I'll hand it in." The door opened a crack and I handed in the cup of coffee.

"Now go away, please."

"Listen, Marsha. You're going to feel better. Piggy has rented the sailboat and we're going down in about an hour. Get yourself ready and I'll call you."

"Will you please go away! Thanks for the coffee."

"I'm going to knock on your door anyway, and if you change your mind, we'll be glad to have you."

It was time to go, and Piggy was ready. I didn't feel all that great and wasn't sure that I was ready. I went next door and knocked on Marsha's door. There was no response, and I didn't push it.

Piggy and I got one of Pete's boys to take us to the dock, and there she sat: a beautiful little fifteen-foot sailboat. The owner ran the bait shop. He said he didn't normally rent the boat, but he understood that I was an experienced sailor and knew that I would enjoy sailing it. I got aboard and started putting up the sails. Piggy is a big man and we almost filled the boat ourselves. If Marsha showed up it would be a tight fit.

I had about finished getting the sails on when Marsha drove up. She looked pretty nice in her bright jogging outfit and some sort of sports hat. I noticed that she was wearing dark glasses. I told her to come aboard, that Piggy would handle the lines. There was no wind at the dock, so I ran the sails up and we were ready. With my back to the dock and my eyes on the lake, I hollered for Piggy to come aboard.

The water was colder than I thought it would be. My glasses hung on the end of my nose, for which I was truly thankful. I noticed that Marsha was swimming toward the dock. Well, at

125

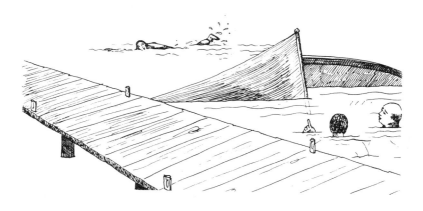

least she could swim; it occurred to me that I hadn't asked her whether she could or not. Piggy was between the boat and the dock, trying to climb up. I don't generally get mad at Piggy, but now I was mad. "What the hell did you do?" I said. One of our spectators answered for him. "He just stepped off the dock onto the edge of the little boat and it went over. He's a big man and it's a little boat." Piggy had gotten out of the water with the help of a couple of bystanders and was sitting on the dock. He was out of breath, but I was not through. "Piggy, dammit, you have been around boats all your life and you know better than to step on the gunwhale of a little boat."

"I'm sorry about it," he said. "But I'm used to bigger boats and I didn't realize this boat was so little and flimsy."

"Well at least go see what's happened to Marsha!"

The dock boy came up to help. "That lady that was with you climbed out, got in her car, and left. She didn't look too happy."

I was still in the water and getting cold. "Well, I'm not too happy either. If you'll help me, we'll get this boat righted and bailed." I stepped on the centerboard and we got the boat righted and tied to the dock.

"We've got an electric pump, and it won't take but a few minutes. I'll look after it, Mister. You'd better go get dried off and get some warm clothes."

The boat's owner looked glum. "I thought you guys knew how to sail," he said.

"The problem wasn't sailing. We never left the dock. I'm going to get some dry clothes, and when I come back we'll check the boat out and see if it's all right. I'll be responsible if there is any damage." His attitude improved.

"I think she's all right," he said, "but I'll check it with you."

We were back in dry clothes pretty soon, but it was obvious that we were not going sailing. The owner had taken the sails off and put the boat back in her slip. "No damage," he said. "I'll give you your money back."

"Why don't we split the money and you give my half to the dock boy. I appreciate his help."

Piggy and I checked out the big outboard, filled the fuel tanks, and otherwise got ready for the trip back to Harrison Bay. I was feeling a lot better, and my hangover was practically gone. Piggy had recovered enough to ask, "By the way, what happened to your girlfriend? She didn't even say goodbye or offer to take us back to the cabin. The dock boy said she'd lost her dark glasses and looked pretty unhappy."

We caught a ride back to the village and got ready to check out. I noticed that Marsha's car was gone and that a maid was cleaning the room. "Did the lady leave any message?" I asked.

"No, sir. She just packed and left."

Somehow this news restored Piggy's good spirits. "What did you expect? The nice lady comes out for a quiet weekend; you pick her up, get her drunk, take her to bed, and then dump her in the lake."

I started to say, "That's not fair," but gave up and packed my bag.

Our group leader said that we would meet at the lock at 2:00 and lock through together for the trip back. Our commander announced that we could proceed at our own pace, and that he would bring up the rear to be certain that all stragglers got home safely. This sounded like a nice thing to do, but we didn't figure we would require his services.

I took the wheel and eased out of the lock when the keeper blew the horn. Piggy sat in the sun with a handkerchief over his bald head. He looked relaxed, but I knew better. I figured that in another fifteen or twenty minutes he would take the wheel and "get this thing going."

&

I imagined Marsha on her way home. She squinted into the autumn sun. Her new sunglasses were gone and the new warm-up outfit, still soaking wet, was in a laundry bag. The new hairdo was gone, too, and so was the sports hat. She had managed a sort of ponytail, which she knew didn't do a lot for her appearance. She said to herself, "Nice, quiet weekend. Just what I needed to think things over. Picked up, plied with liquor, taken to bed, and dumped in the lake. Damn that Uncle Dudley! I'm too old for this kind of stuff. Maybe I ought to go back to Ralph—I'll need to get my hair done first. I'll think about it."

&

We were already well ahead of the fleet when Piggy took the wheel. He fiddled with the controls, wanting to be sure that we were going as fast as we could. I sat in the corner of the cockpit and braced myself just in case.

The boat made a loud noise—the motor raced and then quit. The stern settled down and the following wave came over the transom and into my lap. We were not going to sink, but something pretty bad had happened. Piggy looked surprised and hurt. "I am in the middle of the channel," he said. "Look at those markers."

"We're in the channel, all right, and so is that log—part of which is sticking out from under the boat." There it was, half submerged and still partially under our stern. I shoved at it with the boathook and it floated off. The lower unit of the motor was completely gone, sheared off near the water line. We just sat there for a while, not worrying too much about our predicament, trying to absorb the extent of our bad luck.

In a little while Joe S. came alongside and offered his condolences. Piggy said, "I was in the channel. We hit a submerged log." Joe had his wife and two children with him and was ready to help. "I don't really want to tow you all the way to Harrison Bay, but I have an idea that will probably work better. We're only about a mile from the ferry. I can tow you there. There is a good ramp, and Piggy can stay with the boat while I take Dudley back to Harrison Bay. He can get the trailer and come back and pick up the boat. There shouldn't be any real problem, but it may take a little while." We adopted Joe's proposal without argument, and after a short tow, Piggy tied the boat to a tree near the ferry ramp.

The P-G Special was still hooked to the trailer. I thanked Joe and hoped that it would start. The Special is not one of my favorite vehicles, but it eventually coughed a couple of times and started. Piggy was still sitting in the boat when I got back to the ferry. He looked pretty glum, but we got the boat loaded and headed for home. "Piggy, don't worry too much. I'm going to pay my share of that motor, and I don't think the boat is hurt."

"That motor was nearly new, and the lower unit is gone. I think I know where I can get one from another dealer."

We rode in silence, contemplating our problems. I looked in the rear-view mirror and noticed that our flag was still flying proudly from the top of the cuddy.

129

It was getting a little dark when we got to Ooltowah. I didn't pay much attention to the railroad underpass, and neither did Piggy. I felt the boat hit something. "Damn! Did you take down the flag?"

I didn't bother to answer, because I hadn't. We both got out and there it was, lying in the road. The flagpole still had the flag attached. I folded the flag and put it in my pocket. Piggy picked up the pole and threw it in the back of the truck. Piggy said, "I sure hate to see Hugh."

All Girl Crew

IT CAN GET HOT in north Georgia in August, and it did. I was in my office on Saturday morning—I don't know why; I wasn't working, just looking at the ads in *Yachting* magazine.

"Galesville, Maryland. Charter one of our boats and be your own skipper. Sailing the Chesapeake is easy and fun. Call Hunnicutt Marine."

I picked up the phone and called. Why not? I was not a seasoned skipper—but I owned a fifteen-and-a-half-foot Snipe that I raced on Lake Allatoona with the Atlanta Yacht Club. I hadn't won any races, but I hadn't been last very often either. I'd been to the Chesapeake once before as a crew on a sixty-foot schooner, so maybe I was qualified.

I had a pretty long telephone conversation with the charter people, and they thought it would work out all right. The fact that I was a member of the Power Squadron and taught classes was a big help. Of course, they also wanted to know the name of my bank. Anyway, it was pretty much arranged on the telephone. They had a thirty-foot Atlanta sloop available, which sounded like something I could handle. It had a center cockpit and two cabins, each cabin with a head. I figured if my wife, Evelyn, wanted to, we would take our daughter Dianne and let her take a friend. The accommodations would fit pretty well; I didn't want to be in the same cabin with two teenage girls.

I went home for lunch and told Evelyn to get things ready.

131

She didn't give me much of a problem, and Dianne was de-lighted. She got on the phone immediately, and pretty soon I was talking to Beth's father about her going with us.

"Who wouldn't welcome the chance to get rid of a teenage daughter for a week? You sure you don't want her a little longer than that?" he asked.

"Sam, a week's all I've got. We can pick her up in Atlanta, or you might want to bring her to Rome."

"No. As a matter of fact, we're going to be in Washington that week, and we'll bring her to Annapolis. It ought to work out fine. I'm not sure about the Chesapeake in August, though. It gets hot as hell, and there probably won't be any wind. At least it won't be crowded."

You don't have to pack a lot for a sailboat trip. It's a long way from north Georgia to Galesville, but we made it in one day and checked into a small motel not far from the marina.

The boat looked fine. It was a new design by the late Uffa Fox, who taught Prince Phillip how to sail and sailed with him as crew. He was probably a better teacher than yacht designer, and the Atlanta never caught on as a class. This one, the *Red Fox,* had some peculiarities. A fifteen-horsepower outboard motor sat in the middle of the cockpit in a well. We got used to it, and propped our feet up on it, stumbled over it, and used it to hang things on. I don't know how the rudder was rigged, but the tiller stood straight up in the air and was moved from side to side to steer the boat. After about a week, I got fairly used to it. There was a head in each cabin, located conveniently in the middle of the floor. Privacy was achieved by chasing the other occupant into the cockpit. Two bronze bilge boards replaced the keel and could be cranked up by separate winches located on either side of the companionway. I think in theory the boat was supposed to sail faster with one board down; but my object was not speed and I settled by leaving them both down except when we went aground and had to crank them up.

Evelyn and Dianne got some groceries while I got checked

out by Mr. Hunnicutt. He conceded that the boat was unusual, but thought it sailed fairly well. "It only draws about ten inches with the boards up, so if you go aground, just crank them up, and you should be okay." We finally got underway and headed toward Annapolis. We tried to sail a little, but there really wasn't enough wind, so I finally cranked the outboard, which carried us along at a good six knots. It was still fairly early when we pulled into the Annapolis Yacht Club. I told them I was a member of the Atlanta Yacht Club and checked in with the manager. He found us a nice slip not far from the clubhouse. The manager was very pleasant and said they were delighted to have us and that we could have dinner at the club if we wanted to. He showed me a closet full of odd jackets. "We require a jacket in the dining room after six o'clock, which is not really very practical, since very few visiting yachtsmen carry them. Consequently, we have all of these odd jackets—most of them contributed or discarded by members—and we invite our visitors to wear one for dinner. You may not find one to fit, but that doesn't matter—certainly not as far as we are concerned." I made reservations, and we went off to explore Annapolis.

Beth was a little late, but she and her mother finally arrived about noon. I'm inclined to be a little impatient, so I was ready to shove off when they got there. We promised to take good care of Beth, and were off under motor. There still wasn't any wind, but we headed on out into the bay. I didn't have an itinerary, but thought maybe we would make a big circle clockwise, maybe going into Queenstown, Oxford, and Cambridge before heading back across to Galesville.

Queenstown is located north of the Bay Bridge on the Chester River. Sort of late in the afternoon we had crossed the bay and headed up the river. I thought we would head for Queenstown, although it didn't really matter; we had plenty of food aboard, and I had planned to anchor out anyway. As it turned out, we never did find Queenstown, but we found a nice quiet cove with an old stone pier and a little park. We put out the fenders and tied up. It seemed a good place to spend the night, and we got out and stretched our legs.

I was back aboard thinking about a drink when a man with a young child drove up. He stopped and came over to look at our boat.

"I've got an Alden ketch over at the Kent Island Yacht Club and we do a good bit of sailing. Your boat is unusual to say the least. I don't think I've ever seen one like it," he said.

"I haven't either, and I don't think you're likely to see many of them. It was designed by Uffa Fox, who probably should have stuck to teaching Prince Phillip how to sail. I haven't found out how it sails yet because we haven't had any wind, but it's comfortable enough. I chartered it from Hunnicutt Marine in Galesville."

Sailors love to talk about sailing and sailboats, so he came aboard for a drink. He said he lived in Queenstown, which was only about a mile up the river, and would come back and take us to dinner. We didn't have a heavy schedule, and he and his wife picked us up in about thirty minutes. When I told him I didn't have a jacket, he smiled.

"We have our own jackets," he said. "Don't worry about it."

Dianne and Beth elected to stay on board, and before long we were dining with Mr. and Mrs. William Saunders at the Kent Island Yacht Club.

We ate lots of seafood and drank a moderate amount of whiskey. There was a juke box, and we even danced a little. Dancing is not my thing, and I only mention it because it was that kind of a nice social evening. Bill got to talking about his sailboat and got so enthusiastic that we borrowed a flashlight and went down to the docks. It was a fine-looking boat—a thirty-five-foot Alden ketch—and from what I could see, well maintained. We thought about going aboard, but the girls got a little worried about us and started honking the horn. I don't blame them, but we both got back without falling in the basin, which was remarkable in itself.

❧

The next morning there was a fresh breeze from the north, and after motoring out of the cove I decided to go down through the Kent Island Narrows. Kent Island sticks out in the bay across from Annapolis, and the eastern end of the Five Mile bridge is on the island. The Narrows run from the Chester River between Kent Island and the mainland down to Eastern Bay. The wind was directly behind us, maybe twelve knots, and we went boiling along at nearly hull speed. The Narrows bridge, carrying the same traffic as the big bridge, features a draw, which I understood had restricted opening times because of the traffic. I didn't have the schedule, but the bridge was open and a good bit of traffic was going through the draw. We sailed right through too, waving at everybody. The bridge tender was busy, but my little red boat and our all-girl crew got his attention, and he waved back. I gave the horn a blast, which was unnecessary and probably illegal, and on we went toward Eastern Bay.

I had thought I might go into St. Michaels, which had been highly recommended to us; but that meant going into the Miles River and out of the bay, and the wind was too fair and the day too fine, so we kept going.

My crew had gotten used to the unusual arrangement of the tiller, so that I was able to take a brief nap. This is something that I do very well and as often as I can.

I got out the charts, and we had a brief discussion about our destination. I wanted to go to Oxford, which would be a long haul. We could go through Knapp's Narrows, but Oxford was still a long way off. We decided that maybe we ought to anchor somewhere and go into Oxford the next day.

Tilghman Island juts out into the bay at the point where the Chop Tank River comes in. There is a man-made canal across the island, which saves going south around Black Walnut Point. There was no reason not to go through. At this point, I would like to quote without permission from a well-known nautical guide:

Knapp's Narrows is a busy waterway with steady traffic. There is a marina and a restaurant on the west side of the bridge, which offer free dockage for patrons. The Narrows is crossed by a fast-operating bascule bridge, which customarily opens well in advance so that boats under sail, can, when the tide is right, go boiling through.

I picked up the channel markers for the Narrows and started in under sail. We were on a broad reach and, as the book said, intended to go boiling through the bridge. We did boil up fairly close, blasting on our little gas-can horn, but absolutely nothing happened. I rounded up sharply and made a pretty exciting jibe, but we still had a problem. I hadn't paid much attention to the tide tables, and it was now obvious that the tide was with us. There was not a lot of room for maneuvering, but we made a couple of tacks and seemed to be holding our own. It was past time for starting the motor, and I started it. We kept blowing the horn every now and then, but still nothing was happening with the bridge, so I decided to stop at the restaurant dock.

Deciding to stop and being able to stop do not always go together. There was not enough room to maneuver close to the bridge, so it would have to be a down-wind landing. With the sails down and the motor in reverse, we were still going too fast. It was time for heroic measures. "Get ready, girls, I said. "It's going to be a rough landing. Throw the anchor out over the stern, and give it as much scope as you can. The rest of you try to grab a piling if you can, but don't get hurt." The anchor didn't hold, but it did slow us up, and with everybody grabbing for the dock and the motor in reverse, we stopped just short of the bridge.

There was nobody on the dock to witness our landing, which I thought was just as well. There was nobody in the restaurant either, except a waitress and a man in a fishing cap who was drinking coffee and reading a newspaper. I looked out at the bridge; it seemed deserted and was closed to its fixed height of seven feet. We ordered sandwiches, and I wondered what we were going to do about getting into the Chop Tank. The other customer of the restaurant got up and walked past our booth. "Hope you folks are enjoying the Chesapeake. I'll open the bridge when you're ready to go through. By the way, there's a nice anchorage off to port when you get out of the channel."

୬▲·

It was a nice anchorage, and we had a quiet night. Oxford was once a major seaport and a haven for pirates. Today it is a small, tranquil, lovely town and one of the bay's important yachting centers. Just off the waterfront is a lovely old eighteenth-century inn, which was formerly the family home of Robert Morris, who was called the Financier of the American Revolution. The Tred Avon Yacht Club is located on a point that projects into the Chop Tank where it adjoins the Tred Avon River. I headed for the yacht club, hoping that there would be hot showers available. The yacht club's docks were empty, and we tied up at what appeared to be a transient dock. I noticed that the parking lot was full of small sailboats on trailers and guessed that the yacht club's activities were principally involved with one-design racing. There was a good bit of dock space, but the situation was so exposed that I doubted if any large boats were kept there.

I found my Atlanta Yacht Club membership card and headed for the clubhouse. The door was open, but there was nobody there. We wandered around and used the facilities, but there was no sign of activity. I got some towels from the boat and asked Evelyn to explain my situation if anybody came while I was showering.

Still, nobody showed up, so we decided we would walk into town for some supplies. The main street ended at the yacht club property, so we walked in and found a nice grocery store, maybe half a mile from the club. I hope the eastern shore hasn't changed very much since then, because the people were about the nicest, most hospitable people I've ever run into. When we

finished shopping we had two fairly good-sized cardboard boxes full of groceries; the lady in the store directed that they be put in her car and a pleasant man appeared and drove us back to the dock.

Nobody would admit who did it, but the boxes of groceries were deposited on the top of the sliding hatch. This was not a secure position, and before we could get things stowed, an oyster boat came by, leaving a fair-sized wake. All the groceries went overboard. The light things had been in one box and the cans in another. The box of cans disappeared almost immediately, while the bread, potato chips, and crackers began to float off. The two men in the oyster boat saw what had happened and came back to help. They netted the floating groceries pretty easily, but the canned goods were sunk. I had eaten a few oysters, but didn't know much about how they were harvested. One of the men produced what I learned were oyster tongs, which look sort of like a king-sized post hole digger with handles about ten or twelve feet long. He started groping around on the bottom near the boat and pretty soon had tonged up most of our canned goods, which he deposited on the dock. The labels were beginning to come off, but at least we had most of our food back. The oyster men apologized for their wake, refused our offer of a soft drink, and went on back about oystering.

We decided to stay where we were and walk to town, which wasn't all that far. If you are in the area, try not to miss Oxford. Meanwhile, back at the yacht club, we were still the sole occupants of the dock and in charge of all of the facilities. We probably should have looked for a quieter place to spend the night, since there was a good bit of traffic back and forth, but you get more or less used to the boat rocking a little during the night.

The next morning we left early, planning to go on to Cambridge. I left a thank-you note written on yacht club stationery, and we started for Cambridge under power. Beth had developed a sore throat, and I think she was running a slight fever. We put the motor on full speed and were at the Municipal Yacht Basin in a little more than an hour. Here we put the eastern shore hospitality to another test. Evelyn and the two girls went to look for a doctor to see about Beth's throat. Evelyn was back in a few minutes. The people at the yacht basin office had volunteered to drive Beth and Dianne to a doctor's office some miles away. I stayed with the boat while they were gone, doing a little housekeeping and exploring the area near the docks.

It took a little while, but they finally got back. Beth had a freshly swabbed throat and a bottle of antibiotic pills. We put her to bed and decided that since we had only one more day anyway we would spend the night at the dock and head back to Galesville the next morning.

Beth got a good night's sleep, and we were off early. I had intended to do a lot of motoring, but the wind was still brisk out of the northwest, and gave us a nice reach down the Chop Tank. I decided to hold on out into the bay and around Black Walnut

Point. It was going to be a long sail, mostly on a close reach. Out in the bay it was getting pretty rough, and we were healed over and taking some spray in the cockpit. Beth was feeling better, and I was having trouble keeping her in the cabin. We finally decided that she would be better off in the cockpit, where she would certainly be more comfortable than bouncing around below. Evelyn and Dianne now got some real sailing experience. The wind was about fifteen knots and steady, and the *Red Fox* was behaving nicely. It was just a question of hanging on, and eventually we would get to West River and go up to Galesville.

Eventually can sometimes seem like a long time. I gave Dianne the helm and went below. One advantage of this kind of sailing is that if you pick the right bunk, you're not going to fall out. A few things had fallen on the floor, but nothing serious. I found some leftover ham sandwiches and offered them around with no takers. Even if you don't get sick, continually bouncing around is hard on the appetite. I took a few bites and decided that it wouldn't hurt me to wait, so we all waited, and a good while later I went back on deck and announced that I thought I saw the entrance to the West River.

We turned into the channel. This time there would be no heroics or foolishness. We furled the sails and started the motor. Mr. Hunnicutt was waiting on the dock when I rounded up and made a pretty fair landing. My crew, having returned from a successful cruise, all seemed in better spirits—including Beth—and went off to look for a fast-food outlet. Mr. Hunnicutt and I checked the boat and equipment. I was happy to report that the *Red Fox* had not suffered even a minor scratch. We agreed that a boat with a rudder that sticks straight up out of the cockpit floor and twin bilge boards was not likely to become popular in the United States, and I don't think I've seen another one like it since. We shook hands, and he said I could give him as a reference.

The Rope Ladder

Paul came over from the next slip. "For gosh sakes, Skipper, what are you doing with all of that rope? I know it's a 'line' on a boat, but that looks like rope to me. I'm the expert on marlinspike, and you look like you could use a little help."

"Actually, I'm doing quite well, but I concede that you are the expert. To answer your question, I am constructing a rope ladder for the use of my guests."

Paul sat on the top of the cabin. "This I've got to see," he said. "Why would anybody want a rope ladder when you can buy a good aluminum ladder that is actually climbable? I'm sure you don't intend for anybody to use it, and you are certainly too old to be climbing rope ladders, even if they were properly constructed."

"If you are through insulting my marlinspike ability and my physical condition, I will say a few words in defense of the rope ladder. The rope ladder has a long and honorable history. Queen Elizabeth is reported to have climbed a rope ladder when she inspected Drake's flagship, the *Golden Hind,* and a few years previous to that her father, Henry VIII, is said to have attempted to climb a rope ladder to inspect his flagship when the rope broke and he found himself swimming in the harbor. It was finally necessary to haul him aboard with a block and tackle rigged to the main boom."

"That's enough of that crap, Skipper. You're just making it up."

"I am not. I refer you to an article in the late lamented *Rudder* magazine, which dealt at some length with the history of the rope ladder. It reported that Cleopatra made use of a rope ladder when boarding her barges, and that Jason may have used a rope ladder to get aboard the the *Argo*. You certainly know that Columbus and ships of that era used rope ladders exclusively."

"Okay. Okay. So people used to use rope ladders and you are making one, apparently, to torment your friends."

"I fully intend to use this ladder myself, and if you don't feel *you* have sufficient agility, you had better stay on that cat boat of yours that doesn't have enough freeboard to need a ladder."

I am not much of a carpenter, but I had done a fairly decent job of cutting and sanding five rungs out of a strip of mahogany. Each rung would have a hole bored at each end, and the whole thing would be put together with manila rope. I had seen this in *Popular Mechanics,* and it seemed simple enough.

On a crisp fall day, I sailed out of the club cove and headed for an anchorage across the lake. There was nobody around, but the sun was warm and I thought maybe I would have a last swim before the cool weather. I anchored in about ten feet of water and had a short nap. The nap worked fine, and I was ready to try out my ladder. It was a handsome thing and I admired my craftsmanship. The mahogany rungs, brightly varnished, glinted in the sun, and the new manila rope appeared to be professionally attached to the rungs. I hung one end over a cleat on the stern and jumped in. After swimming around the boat a few times I decided that the time had come, and grasping the rope on either side of the ladder, I stepped on the bottom rung. The rung, which was dangling about a foot below the bottom of the transom, went under the boat. After a few tries, it became obvious that the bottom rung was not going to be of any use, and I finally got one foot on the next rung. I now discovered that I had nothing to hold on to in order to pull myself up. The backstay was a possibility, but I had hung the ladder where it was out of reach. The rope sides of the ladder were of no use, and I was getting a little tired.

A few years previously I could have climbed aboard, but those days were gone and I had a problem. I could swim to shore and walk barefoot in my swimming trunks, looking for help. This didn't appeal to me at all, and I put it at the bottom of my list of alternatives. Rescue appeared possible when two couples came by in a ski boat. I waved frantically, and on their second turn around they saw me and came over.

"What's the matter, Pops? You got a problem?"

"I do have a problem. I am unable to climb back aboard my boat and I would appreciate a little help."

"No problem, Pops," said one, and climbed from the ski boat into the cockpit of *Regardless*. "Now step on the ladder and grab my hand and we will get you aboard."

He did indeed get me aboard, and I was truly thankful.

"If you would like a beer, it will be my pleasure," I said. "You look old enough, and I need one myself."

They joined me in the cockpit and we chatted about boats and water skiing and other such things. When they left, we all shook hands and one of them winked at me and said, "Pops, maybe you ought not to go overboard when you are by yourself— particularly with that rope ladder."

I looked at my ladder and was still proud. There must be a solution to this problem.

The next day, I moved the stern cleat a little to the left so I could grab the backstay with my left hand. By leading the starboard jib sheet back, I had a right-hand hold, and I figured I could stand on the next to the bottom rung and have two pretty good holds. *Regardless* was now in her slip, so I went overboard and on about the second or third try, made it back into the cockpit. No sweat. I now knew I could get back in if I had to. Whether anybody else could do so remained to be seen. I put my ladder back in the locker and awaited my first guest.

The weather in Rome was getting chilly, so I trailed *Regardless* to Panama City and installed her in a slip near the head of Grand Lagoon, just across from Captain Anderson's famous seafood restaurant. The Captain is locally famous, and some-times his customers have to line up in the parking lot. He also maintains a fleet of fishing boats that supply fresh seafood to the restaurant. The food is great, but I am not sure about the Captain's nautical credentials. I've been told that they consist of his having played the banjo in a combo which performed on an excursion boat. Anyway, he runs a good restaurant, and *Regardless* was now within easy walking distance of good seafood.

Mac arrived Thursday afternoon. He had been cruising in the Bahamas on his Albury Bahama sloop, and since he is a bachelor and has plenty of money, he spends most of his time cruising or doing whatever he feels like doing. At one time he was a promising sculptor, but I don't think he has been doing any serious work recently.

He looked at *Regardless* with a critical eye and said, "Is this the boat that got struck by lightning?"

"It is," I answered, "but it made only a small hole in the hull, which I have now repaired with Marine Tex. I do not believe that it constitutes a problem."

"I hope not," he said. "I am due back Monday to meet with some people who may want me to sculpt something. Sculpture clients are few and far between, so I plan to be there. Do you have any particular itinerary for this cruise?"

"Yes," I said. "Tomorrow morning, after a leisurely breakfast at Captain Anderson's, we will leave the slip and head down Grand Lagoon. If the weather is nice, we will go out to the sea buoy and then decide where we are going. If the wind is in one direction, we will head toward Port St. Joe, and if it's in the other direction, we will head toward Destin. We will probably not get to either one."

"That's what I like—firm advance planning. By the way, where do I sleep?"

"You can sleep in the quarter berth if you like, but I think you would be happier in the "V" berth. I'm not giving up my double bunk even for a distinguished blue-water sailor."

"Be a bastard," he said. "About what I expected."

It was a lovely day. Once outside the channel we cut off the sea buoy and headed toward Port St. Joe on a nice broad reach. I thought that at this rate we might even get there before dark. I don't trust my nighttime navigation, although I have navigation lights and two flashlights.

By 3:00 we were not going anywhere very fast. The wind was beginning to head us, and we were almost out of sight of land.

"Mac," I said, "we are four or five miles off shore and headed toward Yucatan. I think it is time to go back while we have some daylight."

"Suit yourself. I've been to Yucatan and don't particularly want to go to Port St. Joe."

I looked at the chart. "It's a long way back to the channel. The chart shows that the old pass runs between Shell Island and the mainland. There is a note dated 1936 that the channel is closed to navigation."

"That doesn't mean us. That means commercial navigation."

"It looks like there may be two or three feet of water on the bar, and *Regardless* draws two and a half with the board up. We might go in and see what it looks like."

The wind was light and I headed in the direction of the old pass. Two small fishing boats with outboard motors came out, apparently without any problem. I waved to one, motioning toward the shore, and he apparently understood me. He held up two fingers and then three which I took to mean two to three feet. There were no breakers, so I told Mac, "Let's try it," and headed toward the spot where the small boats had come out.

We were doing pretty good, moving slowly under sail when we hit the bar. I didn't figure we had any damage, but we were hard aground. The little motor wouldn't be much good. I got out the rope ladder and hung it over the stern. "Come on, Mac, time to get off and push."

We both got off, and without our weight, *Regardless* began to move a little. We both pushed and she moved a little more.

145

"Come on! One more time will do it, I think." We pushed again and she came free. I grabbed the rope ladder and climbed aboard. Mac grabbed the end of the ladder, but we were picking up a little speed and he trailed out behind, holding the last rung. No way he was going to get in with the boat moving.

"Hang on and I'll get the sails down and get you aboard."

We were still moving. Apparently we had cleared the bar and were in deeper water. I pulled the sails down and hollered, "We're past the bar. Come on aboard." Mac tried. He really tried, but it was no good. Mac is a big man—active, but a little past his prime. On the third try, I braced myself and tried to haul him aboard, but it was no use.

Back in the water, Mac lost his cool. "You total, complete, ignorant, stupid bastard," he said, "why don't you have a regular ladder like everybody else? You put me out on a sandbar in the middle of the Gulf of Mexico. I think you did it on purpose. What do you do now?"

"The first thing to do is for you to calm down a little. You're not in any danger—it's just inconvenient."

"Inconvenient!" Mac lost his cool again and seemed unable to talk.

"Try to calm down a little. Shell Island is less than half a mile away. There used to be an old dock near the end of the island where I can tie up and you can walk ashore and get back aboard."

"I'm not sure I want to get back aboard, but go ahead."

I started the outboard and headed for Shell Island with Mac streaming out behind at the end of the ladder.

The old dock was still there—at least enough of it for me to come in and tie up. Mac came aboard without speaking, went below and laid down in his bunk. I went ashore and walked over to the beach. It occurred to me that he might decide to maroon me on Shell Island, but I didn't figure he was really quite that mad.

We spent the night tied to the old dock, and after a couple of drinks and some hot stew things got fairly friendly again.

The next morning the wind was fair and we had a great sail down the bay and up Grand Lagoon. We were back in the slip by mid-afternoon, and things were back to normal. Mac announced that he was going shopping, and I thought it well to let him go. I hung around the marina for a while and then walked over to St. Andrews Park to get a little exercise.

When I returned I saw it glinting in the late afternoon sun—a new aluminum boarding ladder, perched on the transom. Mac sat in the cockpit reading a newspaper. He looked up, smiled brightly and said, "All is forgiven. Look what I bought for the boat. I noticed that you didn't have a ladder."

"It's beautiful, Mac, and I will certainly need it. By the way, where is the rope ladder?"

"Oh, that," he said. "It fell overboard when I was putting the new ladder on the transom. I tried to get it back, but it seemed to be headed to Port St. Joe."

Dinner at Plato's

GEORGE KICKED ONE of the trailer tires, and I thumped the boat. I'm not sure why people do things like that.

"Well, you've hauled that outboard six hundred miles. What are you planning on doing with it?" George lives in Melborne, Florida, and I live in Rome, Georgia. It is about six hundred miles from Rome to Melborne, and I had hauled the outboard all the way.

"I got tired of going up and down Allatoona. I can go the entire length and back in thirty minutes. I thought maybe we could take some trips, maybe on the waterway or somewhere. You live down here, you ought to know some places to go."

George lives on the Indian River, and the inland waterway goes right by his dock. He doesn't go anywhere much because the only boat he has is a Sunfish, which he dearly loves to sail. I don't particularly care for it; you have to bend over too far to keep the boom from hitting you in the head, and you can't see where you are going. The Sunfish may be fun, but you're not going to take any long trips in it.

"There are lots of places to go if you like to ride in a motorboat, which I don't particularly care about, but since you hauled the thing all the way from Rome we might as well go somewhere. The waterway runs up and down in front of my house, and you can go north to New York or south and west to Galveston. If you don't want to go on the waterway, we could go up the Banana River to Port Canaveral and go out in the ocean and bounce around. If you really want to be gutsy, we could go out Canaveral and go down the coast and hope to get in through Sebastian Inlet.''

"The Banana River doesn't sound too bad, but I'll pass on Sebastian. I went out there once on a fishing boat and it scared me to death. Somebody said the current runs out at about seven knots, and the waves break on the bar when it's not even blowing hard. Let's think of somewhere else.''

That night we had a good time studying the charts and road maps. I was sort of in favor of going over to the St. John's River and going down toward Palatka, but George said he had done that.

"Why don't we go over to Okeechobee and come down the St. Lucie Canal to Stuart? We can get on the waterway at Stuart and come back to Melborne.''

My outboard is a good boat—eighteen feet long with a big motor. Without a heavy load it will do nearly forty miles an hour, and it planes comfortably at about twenty-five. On the map it looked like a pretty long trip, but we measured it at about a hundred miles, which would make a nice one-day trip. Evelyn and Nancy declined to go.

"It's too long; it will be too hot and too bouncy. We'll take you to Okeechobee and let you out, and then bring the trailer back home.'' It sounded reasonable, so we planned it that way.

In spite of Mr. Disney and numerous other real estate developers, there is a great deal of Florida still in its natural state. Southwest of Melborne there is a lot of land I would call swamp but which is more politely referred to as marsh or everglades. You can read that the everglades are on the verge of extinction, but it seemed to me that there is a good bit left. North of Okeechobee it's open dairy land. If you drink a glass of milk in Florida, the chances are the cow lives somewhere around Okeechobee.

We went through the town of Okeechobee and arrived at the lake. There was a small combination marina and grocery store where we launched the boat and bought soft drinks and crackers. The fellow at the launching ramp said it was about twenty miles to Port Mayaca, where we would take the St. Lucie Canal. There is not much at Port Mayaca; in fact, you could even miss it if you aren't looking that way. Its notable landmark is a railway draw-bridge that stays open and sticks up in the air.

I was a little disappointed in Lake Okeechobee. It's about thirty miles across in any direction and is the second largest natural freshwater lake in the United States. It is mostly shallow and generally muddy and not very attractive looking. Because of disastrous flooding in past years, the entire lake rim has been built up into a levee, so that it is generally not possible to see the lake at all from any of the highways. From a boat, about all you see is the top of the levee, which looks pretty much the same all the way around. I understand that the water can get awfully rough in bad weather, but we were going to run down the east shore and our weather looked fine. We weren't in a big hurry, so we put the boat on a nice easy plane and headed south. In less than an hour we were at Port Mayaca, where the railway draw-bridge was sticking up in the air. If there is anything else in Port Mayaca, we didn't see it. It's about thirty-eight miles from there to Stuart, and with one lock to go through, we figured to be in Stuart in a couple of hours at most.

The Okeechobee waterway crosses Florida, the eastern end being at Stuart and the western end near Fort Myers. The total length is about one hundred fifty-six miles. The St. Lucie Canal runs from Stuart to Port Mayaca on the lake, a distance of thirty-eight miles. The St. Lucie lock, fifteen miles from Stuart, has a lift of about fifteen feet and is the only lock between Okeecho-bee and the Atlantic Ocean. The canal, which is also the St. Lucie River, is an attractive stream bordered by palmettos, man-groves, and other semi-tropical trees. There are occasional houses, and at Indian Town, a small village on the north side of the canal, there is a good-sized marina catering mainly to bass fishermen. The canal intersects the intra-coastal waterway near

Stuart. We would stay on the canal to Stuart. Past the intersection with the waterway, the St. Lucie inlet leads into the Atlantic Ocean.

᠈᠗

I wanted a rest stop, so we went into Indian Town and stopped at the marina, which is just off the canal. If you ever really want to get away from it all, Indian Town might be the place to go. There is not anything much there, and it's not near anything. The country is mainly citrus groves, dairy farms, and swamp. The man at the marina was helpful and talkative. He topped our tanks and we bought more soft drinks and some suntan lotion.

"What do you folks do around here for excitement?" I asked.

"Well, there isn't much excitement really," he said. "There's a big rodeo once a year, and there's 'gator wrestling at Roy's Bar nearly every Saturday. 'Course, there's a lot of fights, but nobody generally gets hurt too bad. Did have a funny thing, a couple of weeks ago—guy happen through here with a bear named Ginger that he wrestled. They put on quite a show, and there was lots of betting going on. I put a bet on Ginger and won, but lots of folks didn't think it was on the level. After all, he and the bear was traveling together in a pickup truck. I wouldn't want to bet a lot of money on that kind of deal."

It was time to go, and we went on down the canal. The lock was no trouble, and the tender was friendly and helpful. There's a little park at the lock, so we got out and stretched our legs and enjoyed the scenery. I figured we were ahead of schedule and would be in Melborne before dark.

Looking back, I don't see how two grown men could be so stupid. George lives in Florida and ought to know something about the Florida weather. I used to be a Scout master and ought to know that the motto "Be prepared" wasn't adopted for nothing. Other than our fuel tanks, a small anchor, and one paddle, our equipment consisted of two ham sandwiches, a whiskey bottle half-full of water, and some suntan lotion. We were not prepared for anything much.

Coming into Stuart I noticed some cloud build-up in the west. Probably a brief afternoon shower; we could always go in somewhere if we needed to. The boat had a canvas top that hadn't been used in a good while, and there had been some side curtains that were probably still on board. Near Stuart the sky went black and the wind picked up. We slowed down and put up the top; it looked a little ragged, but was better than nothing. George found the side curtains under the floorboards; they looked a little worse than the top. We would not be exactly snug, but would be out of the worst of the rain. It began to rain hard, and visibility got pretty low. An outboard like mine doesn't have windshield wipers, so you just do the best you can.

"George, you are the navigator. We shouldn't be far from the junction with the waterway. We need to watch out for it. I don't want to go out St. Lucie inlet."

We weren't planing now, just mushing along about ten miles an hour, trying to keep dry and see where we were going. George said, "I've been here before. The intersection with the waterway is well marked, and we shouldn't have a problem. I figure it's maybe another two or three more miles."

We kept easing along, not seeing much, looking for the waterway. I began to get a little nervous, but George said we hadn't gone far enough.

"George, I'm getting a little worried, let's stop and look around." I took the motor out of gear and stuck my head out of the side curtain. It wasn't raining quite so hard now, and visibility was a little better. I couldn't see a thing but water.

"You look out and see if you see anything," I said. "We ought to at least be able to see the bank if we are in the waterway. I think we are in the Atlantic Ocean."

"If you are so damn nervous, why don't you go back?"

"I would be delighted to go back if you'll tell me which way is 'back.' I want to get back."

I think George was getting a little disgusted with me. "Well, Florida will be hard to miss. Just head west, and we'll land before long."

"Unfortunately, we don't have a compass, and I don't know west from east." That got his attention.

"I thought you were the founder of the Rome Power Squadron and Educational Officer and all of that business. They ought to take your certificates back, and if I ever get back to Florida, I'm going to write the national office and suggest that you be defrocked."

"George, my sense of humor is as good as yours, but this is not funny. We've got half a tank of gas, and I think we are in the Atlantic Ocean. We don't know which way is back, and I'm gettin' cold and tired. If we just cut the motor off and drift, we may drift out of sight of land and never get back. The weather is going to lift sometime, but we both may be dead of exposure by then."

"You do have an anchor, I guess? Why don't we anchor for a while?"

I did have an anchor—a small Danforth and about fifty feet of line. I threw it overboard; at about forty feet it hit the bottom. "I doubt if it's going to hold with practically no scope, but in this part of Florida I've been told that the bottom drops off very gradually and with a little luck we can work ourselves into shore by sounding with the anchor."

"That must be something you learned in the Power Squadron and never expected to use."

"It's about the only thing I can think of right now, except for praying for better weather or for another boat to come along."

I was beginning to get cold now and was thinking about praying. I've never done much praying—never been against it, just haven't done much. I was sort of getting my prayer together when we heard the big diesel. I put the motor in gear and started toward where we thought we heard the sound. Pretty soon it came out of the mist—a big party fishing boat. The fishermen

154

must have been below, but the captain was at the wheel, apparently trying to figure out where he was going.

"Go over and ask him where we are."

I eased over, cut the motor and waved. He obviously didn't want to stop, but I kept alongside and kept waving and he finally cut his motor. I shouted "Stuart?" and pointed ahead. He nodded and was back on his way. Not much of a conversation, but satisfactory from our standpoint. I tucked our boat in behind the fishing boat—happy to have a guide.

Maybe fifteen minutes later we saw a post with a sign on it. It was a good-sized sign. "Plato's Marina, Bar and Grill—On the Waterway—3 Miles." There was an arrow pointing to our right. We headed toward Plato's. I hoped he had a hot shower.

Plato seemed pleasant. He had bushy hair and a heavy beard. "The showers will cost you a dollar apiece, and you can rent towels for a dollar apiece. Not buy—just rent. I can also sell you a tee shirt at a terrific bargain." He held up a white tee shirt on which was pictured a man with bushy hair and a full beard. It said "Plato." I got two towels and a tee shirt and headed toward the showers. George said, "I'm going to call Nancy and ask her to come after us. It's getting dark, and I'm sure you have no navigation lights. We can come back for the boat tomorrow."

It suited me. I'd had enough boating for the day; maybe for good. "Go ahead," I said.

I stood for a long time in the hot shower. I figured I probably owed Plato at least two dollars for the water.

George stuck his head in. "Nancy and Evelyn are coming after us. It will probably take about an hour."

My new tee shirt felt pretty good, and I rented a third towel to go around my neck. I also bought a pair of socks, and gradually I began to warm up a little bit. Plato said, "The bar is open. You guys look like you could use a couple of drinks." We took his suggestion and sat in the bar. It was a quiet night and Plato joined us.

I felt a little silly when I said it, "You must be Plato?"

He looked around and hesitated. "No, actually I'm not. I bought this place from Plato six months ago and named it the Waterway Inn. For a while I couldn't sell anything to anybody. I finally let my hair grow and grew this beard and everybody thinks I'm Plato. Business is better, but if I ever sell this place, the first thing I'm going to do is get a haircut and shave this damn beard."

We had another drink and told boat stories and other lies. We told Plato about going down to St. Lucie inlet, and George remarked that he had remembered that the intersection was well marked.

"Well it was, but a few days ago a guy in a big motorboat ran over the marker, knocked it down and dragged it away. I think the Coast Guard has put up a temporary marker, but it may not be as big as the one we had. It wouldn't be hard to miss the junction in this kind of weather."

"Not hard at all," I thought to myself. "Even for experienced yachtsmen."

We heard a car drive up. George told Plato we would be back to pick up the boat the next day. We went outside and climbed into the car with the two beautiful young women who had come to rescue us.